EARLY CHILDHOOD
EDUCATION
A Methods and Materials Book

EARLY CHILDHOOD EDUCATION

A Methods and Materials Book

By

HAROLD D. LOVE, Ed. D.

Head, Special Education Department
State College of Arkansas
Conway, Arkansas

and

W. H. OSBORNE, M.A.

Director
Council on Early Childhood Development
Office of the Governor
State of Arkansas

79269

CHARLES C THOMAS · PUBLISHER
Springfield • Illinois • U.S.A.

Published and Distributed Throughout the World by

CHARLES C THOMAS · PUBLISHER

BANNERSTONE HOUSE

301-327 East Lawrence Avenue, Springfield, Illinois, U.S.A.

NATCHEZ PLANTATION HOUSE

735 North Atlantic Boulevard, Fort Lauderdale, Florida, U.S.A.

Library of Congress Catalog Card Number: 75-143747

With THOMAS BOOKS *careful attention is given to all details of
manufacturing and design. It is the Publisher's desire to present books
that are satisfactory as to their physical qualities and artistic possibilities
and appropriate for their particular use.* THOMAS BOOKS *will be true
to those laws of quality that assure a good name and good will.*

PREFACE

Eⁿᴀʀʟʏ ᴄʜɪʟᴅʜᴏᴏᴅ ᴇᴅᴜᴄᴀᴛɪᴏɴ is fast becoming the new rallying point in the American school system. While we have no hesitancy to espouse the claim that early education experiences can have exceptional value, we also wish to introduce a note of caution.

We find throughout the United States that in our school system many children are being excluded, far too many children have "learning problems," there is a growing alienation of people from schools, and discontent between teachers and administrators, teachers and teachers, local schools and colleges, is increasing. These circumstances prevail in states which are only now beginning to consider the educational needs of young children, and these circumstances also prevail in states which have operated early education programs for years.

We offer, then, as a warning, our belief that early childhood programs will not solve the many ills of our schools unless change occurs throughout the educational system. Early childhood programs will not prevent problems if the remaining educational practices continue to create them. Early childhood programs will not enhance children's motivation to learn if subsequent phases discourage motivation. Early childhood programs will not create a sense of belonging if other levels emphasize exclusion or separation.

Certain devotees of early childhood education seem to feel that, given excellent experiences at early levels, the rest of the school program can retain its present mode of operation. This is an excellent way of selling early childhood education, but it is, in our opinion, absolute nonsense.

In this book we have attempted to place early childhood programs in the framework of the total educational sequence. We have done so because, in the education process, events at one level can and do have an impact on events at all other levels. In other words, activities at one level influence activities at both preceding and succeeding levels. Thus, young children in excellent programs will soon learn from older children in less excellent programs that another day is approaching. This awareness may stem from direct interaction among children, from parental attitudes based on observations of the older children, or from both of these. The educational process is a systems process, and we must not lose sight of it.

Early childhood programs should serve as models for all other segments of the educational system. By doing so, variable class standards, alternative teaching strategies, instructional teams, student-teacher planning, and other improved educational practices can appear in all levels of the system. Effective programs for young children—indeed, effective programs for anyone—will require many dramatic changes. This is particularly true in teacher preparatory programs because involvement of local schools and teacher training institutions, early contact with children, and the opportunity for vertical as well as horizontal movement by educational personnel will be required.

A discussion of materials and techniques is presented in this text. The reader is urged to remain aware that the intent of chapters pertaining to these topics is to suggest approaches which will stimulate the interests of children, which will encourage student-teacher planning, and which will permit students to make decisions in the absence of fear that wrong answers will be given. The techniques are presented as starting points and are not to be viewed as a "basic primer" in early education teaching strategies.

We are indebted to many persons: Dr. Tony Milazzo, University of Michigan; Mrs. Eileen Lehman, U.S. Office of Education; class members of Special Education 6380 during the fall semester 1969-70; Mrs. Hoyt Allen for her review under the most pressing circumstances; and especially to Mrs. Debbie Osborne and Mrs. Loretta Farris.

Mrs. Katty Crownover should be singled out for her diligent work in typing the manuscript, and also for proofreading.

The authors wish to thank Sue Love and Molsie Osborne for their help in the preparation of the manuscript.

H.D.L.
W.H.O.

CONTENTS

Page

Preface .... **v**

Chapter

1. IMPLICATIONS OF EARLY CHILDHOOD EDUCATION 3
2. CLASSROOM ECOLOGY 17
3. THE SCHOOL—PAST, PRESENT, AND FUTURE 37
4. READINESS 53
5. TECHNIQUES FOR TEACHING MATHEMATICS TO
    PRESCHOOL CHILDREN 63
6. PREPARING CHILDREN FOR READING 72
7. PARAEDUCATIONAL PERSONNEL 82
8. HEALTH AND SAFETY 94
9. ART 102
10. COMMUNICATIONS 110
11. SOCIAL LIVING 116
12. MUSIC IN THE PRE-ELEMENTARY SCHOOL 121
13. LANGUAGE PROBLEMS IN THE FIRST FEW YEARS OF LIFE 127

Index 139

EARLY CHILDHOOD
EDUCATION
A Methods and Materials Book

Chapter 1

IMPLICATIONS OF
EARLY CHILDHOOD EDUCATION

IF EDUCATION IS DEFINED AS "the process by which one acquires and learns to adapt knowledge," it follows that the goal of education is to prepare all individuals to be active learners throughout their life spans. The challenge facing American education is the need to use the school situation as a protective, yet nourishing environment which encourages students to organize experiences, activities, and facts into a framework which will enable them to deal adequately with new experiences and new activities they are certain to encounter.

We believe this requires formal educational programs to change emphasis from factual instruction to curricula based on the principles that, in the last analysis, the responsibility for learning resides in the learner, not in the teacher. The child entered the school as a very active learner and, if given the opportunity, will continue to remain as such; and the objectives of the school must be child-centered, rather than school-centered. We maintain, for example, the objective of a first grade class should not be for the class to read at an average first grade level, but, rather, to enable each child to use reading as a means of enhancing his personal life, and as a way of increasing his future opportunities.

The thesis of this and subsequent chapters is that the attitude which implies the school, and only the school, knows what a child should learn, how he should learn it, and when he should learn it, must be changed to reflect an awareness that children learn at different rates, have different backgrounds, have varied interests, and must have the opportunity to play an important role in determining educational programs if these programs are to be appropriate to their needs. We stress student-teacher planning of study units because schools should be places where students have the opportunity to plan, and see the results. This would acknowledge that children will make mistakes.

[3]

However, it will also permit students to profit from these mistakes. Presently, in schools, it seems that to be right is imperative—to be wrong is disastrous.

This approach to education requires teachers to assume the posture of becoming persons who are monitors of the learning process; who emphasize method rather than content; who stress prevention, rather than remediation; who are humanistic; who seek to prevent learning problems from arising by finding the appropriate match between child and task, and who purposefully seek to develop strategies which turn kids on. Educational programs which prepare children for a world which will exist twelve to fourteen years hence must begin by accepting the child where he is now, rather than where he is assumed to be, and must progress in meaningful steps.

American education today appears to concentrate on the perpetuation of a way of life considered desirable by the middle class. In fact, the most crucial member of the educational system—the teacher—is perhaps the most middle class of all, and consciously or unconsciously measures her students by her own standards. The dilemma is that middle class values have come to be accepted as given and, when challenged, practitioners of these values neither understand the nature of the challenge nor respect the right of the challenger to do so.

This is not to say middle class values are wrong *per se*—rather, that individuals should know why certain values have emerged, to whom they apply, and why they may not be accepted by everyone.

In essence, we are arguing that schools should prepare individuals to understand, not simply accept, value systems which underlie their behavior. We also believe that if schools can help young people to be more curious, more interested in learning about their environments, more able to cope with new experiences, then these understandings will emerge.

Pre-elementary education for children between the ages of two and six is now being given considerable attention because it seems reasonable to claim that pre-elementary education is desirable for all and, under proper circumstances, can increase the opportunity for children to learn more, and to learn it more quickly. It is certainly obvious that man's knowledge is increasing at a rapid rate, and if children are to cope with their future environments, educational programs must necessarily provide stimulation which will both encourage and enable children to learn more at progressively earlier ages.

We propose in this text to discuss the need for pre-elementary education because it is believed that strengthening educational programs in the early grades will produce significant positive improvements in later grades. Further, it is assumed that the most practical way to introduce a humanistic approach to education at any level will be through a humanistic program introduced at early grade levels.

Pre-elementary school situations in America are usually nursery schools and kindergartens where the child is exposed to group interaction, learns to be cooperative, and is prepared for entrance into elementary school. Todd and Hefferman (1967) suggest several factors in modern American environments which explain the need for the establishment of kindergartens and nurseries. One important factor is the move away from the cities. People living in the suburbs often have many things in common, not the least of which being children of comparable ages. Suburban communities lend themselves to gatherings of parents wherein they can discuss mutual problems of child-rearing and pre-elementary school.

Another factor underlying the need for pre-elementary school education rests on the numbers of mothers seeking to enter the labor market. Day care programs are permitting many mothers—especially those from disadvantaged backgrounds—to work outside the home. Some provision, obviously, must be made for the children of these mothers, and day care centers, kindergartens, or nursery schools present desirable choices.

Day care centers are expected to mushroom as the result of passage of Title IV, Sections A and B of the 1967 Amendments to the Social Security Act. Section A permits federal matching funds to be awarded to day care programs. Section B, which is the basis for the Work Incentive Program, permits funds to be expended for day care services for mothers from poverty backgrounds who elect to enter training programs. These and other federal funds will permit establishment of day care and child care programs throughout the country. In addition, industry is becoming more aware that adequate day care programs for children of mothers in its employ reduce absenteeism, as well as improve employer-employee relations.

There is no doubt that the number of day care programs will increase. However, there is considerable anxiety concerning the quality of the programs which will be developed. At the same time, however, the opportunity does exist to use day care and child care services as a means of improving the experience level of disadvantaged children in order to increase the likelihood of successful performance when they enter the first grade. Further, these centers offer teachers and parents the opportunity to understand better the aims and objectives of programs for young children.

Day care centers and kindergarten programs can be of singular benefit to economically and socially disadvantaged children. It is likely that in day care centers supported by state and federal funds, the majority of children will be from low-income families. Under proper circumstances day care programs have an excellent potential to assist these children. On the other hand, under less favorable circumstances, certain problems may arise. One such problem is the possibility that day care programs may place young children in the precarious situation of living in a school environment which is totally different from the home environment.

What we are saying is that children may be exposed to, or participate in, activities in day care programs which are the exact opposite of activities conducted in home situations. For example, disadvantaged children may be taught to use forks in day care programs, when at home there are no forks. They may be taught to use a napkin, whereas their families have never heard of napkins. They may be taught to fold up their pallets and place them neatly away, while at home they sleep on the floor. These differences can easily place children in the position of seeing their families in the worst possible light.

As a safeguard, we emphasize the need for the inclusion of parents —especially from low socioeconomic groups—in day care centers. This can serve as a learning experience for both parents and day care workers. It permits parents to see what the program is all about, and enables day care workers to make adjustments in the program. Hopefully, the involvement of parents, and the acceptance of parents by day care workers, will minimize the potentially negative impact of the day care environment on the child's perception of both himself and his parents.

We caution the reader, therefore, to remember that in discussing and planning pre-elementary school educational programs, it is easy to concentrate on the three-to-six-year-old group and, in the process, overlook broader aspects of the entire situation. These aspects involve the need for establishment of programs of adult involvement because the child receives a direct benefit from the education of his parents. In the remainder of this and in subsequent chapters, therefore, it is assumed that the various activities which will be discussed, with respect to the nature of pre-elementary school programs, predicates an active involvement of parents.

This rapid growth of pre-elementary schools, both in number and variety, may result in considerable waste unless there is greater coordination of the goals of different programs dealing with young children. The Coordinated Community Child Care (4-C) concept is an excellent approach to the consolidation and subsequent coordination of services for young children.

The intent of 4-C programs is to encourage public, private, and interested persons to unite under a single banner and, thereby, voluntarily agree to (in a sense) pool the resources and funds of separate programs. If the 4-C concept is realized, it seems rather obvious that much duplication of effort will be eliminated, and that better services —from both an economic and quality vantage point—for young children will result.

THE DISADVANTAGED

Well-planned and operated pre-elementary education programs will eventually benefit all young children. An immediate concern, however, is to assist children from low-income families (i.e., disadvantaged children). The term "disadvantaged" has come to have an important meaning to our educational programs. More on this later. First, we should examine some typical thoughts regarding disadvantaged children.

Disadvantaged students often fail to receive their full measure of educational opportunities because of certain factors in the environment which limit the development of their potential. Approximately one-third of the disadvantaged will never finish high school (Bloom, Davis, and Hess, 1965).

If there is a single common denominator of deprivation, it is probably an economic one. Poverty is a worldwide factor and everywhere tends to set the poor apart. The poor are set apart by factors of isolation, economic life, home and family life, attitudes and orientations, education, and nonacceptance by other classes.

The poor are isolated—in cities, in schools, and in churches. Much of this has been caused by middle class migration from the city at a time when the poor are migrating to the city.

The migration patterns to and from the city pose serious problems for urban educational programs because the standards—especially for intercity schools—remain the same even though there is a substantial shift in the makeup of the school population.

In recent years, there has been a significant increase in the number of persons from rural areas who have been displaced from employment because of farm mechanization, or the lack of opportunity for employment as unskilled or semiskilled workers. These persons have lived in poverty circumstances all their lives; have little, if indeed any, formal education, and are not prepared to enter any form of employment which requires specialized training. When children from these families enter a formal education program which emphasizes academics and stresses a college preparatory program, it seems fair to assume that failure is their almost inevitable destiny.

Home and family life of the poor is characterized by a lack of privacy, unsanitary conditions, and unsafe housing. The poor virtually are never involved in community activities, and the family becomes the major sustaining unit in a young child's life. At the same time, however, there are many forces which tend to destroy the solidarity of this family. Alcoholism and physical violence are common, male figures are frequently absent or become negative models for children, contrasts in ways-of-life are readily discernible, and there is a development of attitudes by young people which differ from those of adults. Generally, there is a growing distinction between the opinions and attitudes of young persons and of adults. Among poor people—especially blacks—this divergence is particularly acute.

The poor are oriented to the present. Needs are such that immediate gratification becomes the way of life. Since tomorrow is likely to be only a continuation of today, long-range goals are impossible.

Pessimism colors their thinking toward themselves and the rest of the world.

When a child from such an environment enters school, he will likely be severely handicapped because of his past experiences. Generally, he will have poor health, poor school attendance, inadequate food, and a limited range of experiences; and, to complicate his problems, teachers' expectations are likely to be based on intelligence quotient or achievement test results. The child responds to these expectations through poor grades, unpleasant habits and manners, improper clothing, and lack of cleanliness so that before long, he is acting just like everyone expects him to act. The vicious cycle has begun.

He probably will not finish high school, and will assume his predestined role in doing his part in continuing the depressive cycle for his offspring.

The recognition that disadvantaged children had "unique" educational problems led American education to begin developing programs for disadvantaged children. The passage of the Elementary and Secondary Education Act (ESEA) in 1965 provided funds for local schools to finance special programs for disadvantaged children. The nature of the act (Title I, ESEA, provides funds solely for programs dealing with disadvantaged children), coupled with the general tendency to categorize groups, resulted in programs for disadvantaged children being viewed as distinct from programs for other children. The tragedy resides in this event because it reflects an emphasis on remediating problems in order for disadvantaged youth to cope with the regular academic program of the school. We argue that more significant results would occur if funds for programs for disadvantaged children were used to improve teaching styles, establish variable standards within classrooms, and, in summary, attempt to improve teaching strategies so all children could benefit.

The impetus to compartmentalize or categorize students on the basis of economic factors stresses the differences, rather than the similarities, of children. As a result, disadvantaged children are viewed as not having learned enough, or as having learning problems because they are disadvantaged. This position ignores the fact that disadvantaged children are forced to learn to master their environment if they are to survive. Granted, the learning of these children differs from children of middle class or different socioeconomic backgrounds. However, the important fact is that disadvantaged children are forced to learn to cope with their environment—an environment which, quite obviously, is very real and meaningful to them.

The point is that disadvantaged children are like other children because they are active learners, and because they have developed communication skills even though what they have learned, and the communication skills they have developed, may not be the same as the learning and language development of children from other socioeconomic backgrounds. We conclude, since this is the case, that the responsibility rests on the school program to utilize factors in the disadvantaged child's environment as springboards to the learning of other skills which will enable him to improve his station in life.

Bereiter and Engelmann (1966) state that the differences in intellectual ability are always poorer among the disadvantaged, especially in those areas of intellectual functioning more indicative of school success, and that disadvantaged children have poor language development, subnormal reasoning ability, and an inability to manipulate symbols. Some areas of performance by disadvantaged children, however, show no significant retardation. The areas are immediate memory span and ability to master specific rote-learning tasks.

A study by Aldrich at Vanderbilt University (1969), concerning the effect of an experimental language development program on raising IQ levels, showed some interesting results. The subjects were preschool Negro children ranging in age from two-and-one-half to five-and-one-half years. The control group was enrolled in a traditional kindergarten. Both groups showed IQ gain by the end of the training period, but the experimental group in the language development program gained on the average of 15 IQ points. It was also noted that younger children exhibited greater gains than older children, and when divided into brighter and slower groups, greater gains were made by the slower group.

This study indicates that special pre-elementary school education, as compared to traditional kindergarten programs, has more potential to prepare youngsters for elementary school. It also exhibits the extent to which intelligence (or at least the kind related to school success) can be broadened. When we take into account all the possible sources of error in an intelligence quotient and relate it to the average IQ gain of 15 shown in the above study, a child could easily be changed in classification from dull to normal, or even to bright normal. It is conceivable that a child can be changed from a classification of border-line retardation to a classification of average. One can only guess as to the extent a higher classification would influence his first grade per-formance if his teacher develops a favorable attitude in her expecta-tions of his behavior.

Hopefully, it will become more generally accepted that many differ-ences shown by children in early elementary grades are due more to the amount and quality of experiences between birth and school-age, than to a basic and never-changing intelligence quotient.

Learning requires sensory experiences, yet many disadvantaged chil-dren, for example, fail to receive sensory stimulation that many middle class parents almost accidentally provide their offspring. Learning can be impaired by improper functioning of one or more of the sense organs, or it can be impaired by a vacuum-like environment, even if all the sensory perceptors are potentially perfect.

New experiences seem to be meaningful only to the extent that they can be related to past experiences. New material can be quite be-wildering and frustrating if it cannot be related to anything one sees, hears, or feels. It is easy to imagine how a child could quickly lose interest in learning if it makes no sense to him. An adult can compen-sate for the lack of knowledge by acquiring it, provided he feels it worthwhile. It would appear that a ghetto youngster, for example, would be unable to grasp the importance of such long-term thinking.

The development of speech can be shown to be affected significantly by conditions in the home (Bloom, Davis, and Hess, 1965). Middle class parents ensure proper and rapid development of language in their children by their willingness to talk freely. Even before a child is able to do anything for himself, words are likely to accompany such acts as feeding, changing diapers, getting ready to go riding, or putting the child to bed. However, under conditions of cultural deprivation, fewer words will be used to convey thoughts. Monosyllables, grunts, and gestures are more likely to be the basic form of communication. It is assumed this is true because the parents lack verbal ability and possibly do not have the energy.

Baratz (1968-69) takes exception to the implication by psychologists that the language of Negro ghetto children is "underdeveloped" or in any way lacking in ability to communicate (at least with other ghetto dwellers). She further implies a naivete on the part of the psychologists resulting from lack of knowledge of Negro culture. It is her feeling that the language of the culturally deprived Negro child should in no way be considered inferior, only different. She does, however, recognize a need for "standard" language for contact with the rest of society. It should be taught not to change or replace the person's basic language, but to supply him with another way of speaking for those occasions when it is necessary or desirable.

The disadvantaged child must be made capable of getting along in "standard" America. This incompatibility is resulting in poor school grades, a feeling of inferiority, and resentment developing into hostility. By dropout time, there is likely to be a full-blown feeling of alienation, a bitterness and defeatism that results in unhappiness, continued poverty, and crime.

Job requirements are becoming more complex and require a higher level of mental functioning. The multiplying effects of cultural deprivation and higher job requirements compel schools to cease being concerned primarily, if not exclusively, with those who are likely to seek further academic training. Techniques must be instituted which permit all students to develop to a point approaching their potential. That is, we in education must no longer be content with praising ourselves for our successes while, at the same time, we ignore our failures.

Making schools accessible to virtually everyone is not an answer to the problem of salvaging the culturally deprived. What is needed, according to Bloom, Davis, and Hess (1965), is "a system of compensatory education which can prevent or overcome earlier deficiencies in the development of each individual."

Implementing a pre-elementary school program for the disadvantaged calls for the guarantee that basic needs are met. A child cannot concentrate on abstract problems or think in terms of long-range goals if his stomach is empty, his mouth hurts from decayed teeth, or he cannot see the chalkboard. A reasonable degree of physical comfort is imperative for desired growth to occur.

It seems the first condition to be met with, then, would be guaranteeing the provision of his basic needs. It is suggested by Bloom, Davis, and Hess (1965) that if a proper diet, adequate health care, and sufficient clothing cannot be provided at home, then these areas are rightfully the school's responsibility. If a child decides his basic needs cannot be met, he is likely to adopt a fatalistic attitude which will affect all areas of his life, and this attitude becomes even more fatalistic should the child feel his parents (or those adults in his home environment who look after him) have the same attitude. The school, then, faces the task of providing children with a rich variety of experiences so these children can believe there is a better life, and that his efforts will be worthwhile.

After insuring that basic needs are met, a program recommended by Rees (1968) may begin. Here, the teacher takes the child at his present level—noting his degree of readiness and maturity, and taking into account the child's immediate environment and culture—and guides him step-by-step toward gaining broader concepts and deeper understandings.

Todd and Hefferman (1967) have suggested ways in which children can develop in a pre-elementary school group. The first area of development is as an individual person. The pre-elementary school group can assist one in developing personality and learning to be happy within the bounds of the expectations of society. Social development, or learning the value of other peoples' rights, is of prime importance. Intellectual development, at least to the extent that it enables a child to meet the challenge of more formal schooling, is another goal. An additional concern, physical development, can be implemented by vigorous physical activity and training in good health habits. Finally, emotional development is important. It has long been recognized by psychologists that emotional patterns are established early in life, because only the home has more effect on emotional development than the preschool group.

Dr. Maria Montessori has demonstrated the value of pre-elementary education, first with handicapped children and later with normal children. The techniques she developed still have exceptional merit.

According to Montessori (1914), there is an orderly process through which the minds of children can be developed as efficiently as their physical bodies. Scientific knowledge has lowered infant mortality and greater knowledge of nourishment, and care makes children healthier and more robust than ever. Parents through the ages have successfully raised children, and through experience and knowledge have done many things right. However, much more satisfactory results accumulate from the scientific method. It was Montessori's contention that the mind would develop more rapidly and efficiently by the application of certain principles of learning.

Dr. Montessori's attitude toward the innate tendency for good and evil in human beings certainly favored the good. She contended that those behaviors often classed as "evil" in children are so-called only because of the annoyance caused to adults. Actually, the child in the process of developing is learning by exploring his world. With Montessori's method, the child is allowed "absolute freedom" through organized work. Beginning at age three, Montessori's children received motor education, sensory education, and language through use of such apparatus as cylinders, cubes, boards with rough and smooth surfaces, weighted wood tables, colored tablets with varying shades of colors, and geometric figures of varying shapes and sizes. Language was taught by naming objects, recognition, and pronunciation.

Even today, the results of these sensory stimulating devices determine whether a child is ready by elementary age, or before, to take on the higher aspects of education—reading, writing, and numbers.

Horns and Cowles (1967) feel that pre-elementary education should build a foundation which will enable deprived children to cope with the larger society and make possible the development of innate potential. For this to be done, an impact must be made on parents because so much is determined by home background. As far as what is presented to the child is concerned, Horns recommends exposure to art, music, creative play, verbal expression, vocabulary improvement, listening and auditory skills, visual discrimination and perception, and cognitive development. Additionally, good health habits should be taught along with motor coordination and rhythm development.

In a very similar fashion, Rees (1968) states: "Every indication points to a program beginning with the young child of age three or four and preparing him through basic experiences in the process of living that will assure him of success later in the educational process." Rees feels that early educational exposure will help prepare the child by helping him understand himself and others, providing him with experences whch will help him understand future situations, and expediting emotional growth through satisfying experiences with music, poetry, stories, color, rhythm, and friendships. As did Horns, Rees feels that parent involvement is essential for success in pre-elementary education.

There are existing pre-elementary educational programs throughout America which reflect some kind of need for an early program. Needs are determined by the type of community and makeup of the population. Most pre-elementary school programs appear to be classifiable as to nursery school or kindergarten. Often the main purpose of nursery school is to enable working mothers to have supervision of their children. To a certain extent, kindergarten also fills this need but, in addition, usually places more emphasis on preparation for elementary school work.

The advantages of pre-elementary school education for the physically and mentally handicapped have been pointed out as an important contribution toward neutralizing the negative effects of a disability on personality, social relationships, and job satisfaction.

The most important immediate implication of pre-elementary education for normal children, the disadvantaged, and the physically handicapped is the enabling of each individual to realize more fully his real potential for learning and becoming productive. The broader prospect for the future is a nation of cooperative and productive citizens, not perfect in all ways but capable of understanding and dialogue, and able to meet realistically the requirements of living.

REFERENCES

Baratz, J. C.: Language in the economically disadvantaged child: a perspective. *Journal of American Speech and Hearing Association, 10* (4):143-145, 1968.

Baratz, J. C.: Language and cognitive assessment of Negro children: assumptions and research needs. *Journal of American Speech and Hearing Association, 11* (3):87-88, 1969.

Bereiter, C., and Engelman, S.: *Teaching Disadvantaged Children in the Preschool.* Engelwood Cliffs, Prentice-Hall, 1966.

Bloom, B., Davis, A., and Hess, R.: *Compensatory Education for Cultural Deprivation.* New York, Holt, Rinehart and Winston, 1965.

Cowles, M. (Ed.): *Perspectives in the Education of Disadvantaged Children.* Cleveland, World Publishing, 1967.

Davis, H., and Silverman, R.: *Hearing and Deafness.* New York, Holt, Rinehart and Winston, 1965.

Hickerson, N.: *Education for Alienation.* Englewood Cliffs, Prentice-Hall, 1966.

Montessori, M.: *Dr. Montessori's Own Handbook.* New York, Schocken Books, 1967 (first published 1914).

Rees, H. E.: *Deprivation and Compensatory Education.* Boston, Houghton Mifflin, 1968.

Todd, V. E., and Hefferman, H.: *The Years Before School.* New York, Mac-Mifflin, 1967.

Chapter 2

CLASSROOM ECOLOGY

W<small>E BELIEVE</small> it is appropriate to expand certain points made previously because early childhood programs represent a frontier in education. Hopefully, from this land, we can draw teaching strategies, refine teacher preparatory programs, create a climate which encourages receptivity to new ideas and new approaches and, as a consequence, improve educational opportunities for all children — preschoolers through university graduate students.

Preschoolers are not university graduate students in miniature, and university graduate students are not mature preschoolers. At the same time, however, there are similarities. Both are modified by experiences; both must assume active roles if learning is to occur; both need teachers who are sensitive to individual needs, goals and objectives; both need the opportunity to explore, to reach independent judgments, to question the "why" of activities, to make independent decisions; both must feel that there is a place for them in the educational system's scheme of things; and both must be regarded as individual persons who have dignity, who possess rights, and who are entitled to respect.

Early childhood programs can serve to emphasize that students are people and should be treated as such. They should not be "conned" or brutalized (directly or indirectly), or outgamed in games which are stacked against them in the first place. Instead, children—indeed everyone—should enter into educational programs which enable them to become persons who are prepared to assume productive roles in society, who can cope with life, and who can improve opportunities for others.

This leads to a review of various activities and developments in education.

A REVIEW

It is only natural that efforts to treat divergent educational needs led to the compartmentalization of segments of the school population.

[17]

Thus, the recognition that certain children were unable to compete in regular classroom situations prompted the creation of special education classes. These classes, for the most part, were for children who were referred to as mentally retarded, emotionally disturbed, or as suffering from various other handicapping conditions. These classes served as springboards for the creation of other programs for specific groups of children—"gifted," "average," "below average" and for "children from disadvantaged backgrounds." The variety of abilities and interests in classroom situations suggested that greater instructional efficiency would result if children were grouped according to ability. Such grouping was viewed as a means of restricting the range of talents with which a teacher must deal, of enabling teachers to base standards on anticipated performance levels, and of placing students with special learning problems in classrooms managed by teachers with specialized training.

At first glance, it seems plausible that special classes should be established and special programs created. However, it is time that other approaches should be considered. Special classes and special programs are justified on the basis that, without them, children are unable for various reasons to compete with other children. The question which needs to be asked is, "Compete on what basis?" If competition is based on ability to meet unitary standards in classrooms, we suggest that it is infinitely more appropriate to alter classroom standards than to create special programs for children for whom the standards do not apply. The authors suggest that since we now accept the fact that there exists a diversity of needs, attitudes and interests in our society, we should focus our efforts to permit these diversities to exist in regular classroom environments.

The attempts to restrict regular classrooms to children who can compete, with respect to single standards, deny the multifarious standards of the community. In our opinion, then, education should spend less time on creating "special programs" for "special students," and devote its energies and resources toward the creation of classroom environments which allow for the broad range of learning, behavioral needs, and interests of students. This would emphasize that all children have as much value in the classroom as they do in society at large.

Homogeneous grouping recognizes the process of progressive achievement decrement—the process wherein students who are behind when they enter the first grade tend to be further behind at the end of the second, still further behind at the end of the third, and, ultimately, so far behind that withdrawal from school is often the only alternative. Usually, grouping is based on some assessment of achievement level, and those who "test out" at equivalent levels are placed in the same group.

Certain conclusions are then drawn concerning each group. The lower group, for example, is usually assumed to be behind. This poses a problem because the teacher is likely to develop the expectancy that the "behind group" is likely to remain so. This raises the paradox wherein children are placed in a group in order for them to correct "deficiencies," but the nature of selection and the concomitant teacher attitude may reduce the chance the group will overcome these deficiencies. It is, therefore, possible that the grouping process will contribute to the very problem it is designed to solve.

The thought that students can be grouped into homogeneous units is more of a myth than a reality. It is a myth because grouping techniques merely control certain variables, and the effectiveness of this control is open to question. Grouping based on achievement test results postulates the accuracy of the tests, assumes that background experiences are constant, and that questions mean the same thing to all persons who are writing the examination. Since these assumptions may not be valid, it follows that decisions based on them may be invalid.

Even if it is possible to control the variables which determine group assignment, the group is still not homogeneous with respect to factors which underlie achievement—interests, motivation, parental attitudes, peer acceptance, social class status, and a variety of other factors too numerous to mention.

Our point is that we assume groups to be homogeneous because of performance levels on some criterion (perhaps even criteria), but that, in reality, the group is heterogeneous. Educational programs based on the assumption of homogeniety of a group can, therefore, be challenged rather seriously as to appropriateness to the needs of individual children.

We believe homogeneous grouping was a response to a need, but that it was an inaccurate response and more viable alternatives are mandated. Unfortunately, however, it appears that efforts to categorize students are on the increase. From a historical perspective, we have tended to identify groups and develop crash programs to solve the problems we thought existed. Thus, we discovered "juvenile delinquents" and set programs for them, "emotionally disturbed" and set programs for them, "mentally retarded" and set programs for them, "gifted" and set "enrichment" programs for them. Now, we have programs for "disadvantaged children." It is as if we discovered all at once that there were poor people and that something needed doing.

Target schools were identified, special teacher training programs were instituted, and the effort to correct educational deficiencies was launched. The effort accepted the validity of the main thrust of educational programs—preparation for college admission—and programs for the disadvantaged were slanted toward remedial or compensatory efforts so these students could, along with all others, be ready for college admission.

We argue that programs should not be designed, for example, to provide remedial or compensatory assistance to disadvantaged students so they can overcome certain academic deficiencies or meet the standards or requirements of the educational system, but rather that all programs should be based on the need to assist all students to come to better grips with real life situations. Such programs should attempt to assist children to learn and develop skills so they can enrich their lives, rather than attempt to lull children into a pattern wherein they can conform to some single classroom standard.

More specifically, we believe that the current practice—to dichotomize school populations into disadvantaged and nondisadvantaged groups and treat them accordingly—poses more problems than solutions.

IMPLICATIONS

1. The practice implies that the groups are uniform or homogeneous—that is, by the mere fact that children meet certain economic criteria, they possess similar learning and behavioral needs. Moreover, programs for children from economically deprived backgrounds seem to reflect an attitude that failure is the manifest destiny of these chil-

dren. Further, it appears an attitude prevails to the effect that after failure occurs, then, and apparently only then, the school can do something about it—through remedial or compensatory programs.

2. The practice suggests little or no interaction should transpire between the two groups. This is especially interesting if such claims as "disadvantaged children have limited communication skills, are present-oriented, respond only to sounds of authority," and a host of other factors are true. It is also interesting because these factors seem to suggest that interaction among groups will be of significant value.

3. The practice assumes academically oriented educational programs for nondisadvantaged children are appropriate. We say this because the main thrust of remedial and compensatory programs for the disadvantaged is to assist them in coping with academically oriented programs. Thus, we know the typical school program produces failure (parenthetically, we do not really know if it produces success), and we react by treating its failures—not the process which produced these failures—unlike most other treatment programs which seek to discover and correct causes rather than treat symptoms.

4. The practice assumes programs for nondisadvantaged children are adequately financed. We draw this conclusion from the comparison of federal expenditures for educational programs for the disadvantaged with expenditures for activities related to the total educational process (library, educational media, teacher salaries, equipment, etc.).

5. Since the practice concentrates on failures (i.e., "waste products"), the element of accountability is removed from the educational system. As long as education is not compelled to examine why failures exist, or as long as it is permitted to shift blame to children for its limitations, then for that long can the system avoid looking into itself to discover why children drop out, lose interest, cease being creative and turn to other means, such as drugs, in order to be "turned on." True, educators—particularly administrators—must report to school boards and to various elements of the community. In the process, they overlook accountability to treat students with dignity and respect, to provide programs so that even the "weakest" have a vital part to play, and to provide growth-fostering environments.

Higher education is also in line for the charge that it operates in a splendid absence of accountability. Prospective teachers are taught by instructors who have long forgotten what classrooms (both local schools and their own) are all about. Admission to the "professional" aspect of teacher preparatory programs is centered on how well the student has responded to the system and, in the process, disregards how well the system has responded to the student.

When one considers the rigidity of education departments toward change, it is of little wonder that local schools are also rigid. When one considers how little time is spent in permitting prospective teachers to deal with children in real situations, it becomes understandable that the educational systems feels itself competent to tell a six-year-old child he is a failure, immature, a slow learner, and a host of other things.

These five points lead to our contention that education should not categorize students on the facility of these students to compete with the educational program as it currently operates.

Alternatively, we maintain classrooms and schools are microcosms of society, and that the divergency and differences which exist in society have correlates in classroom and school environments. Consequently, the educational system should ensure that classroom activities are germane to a variety of interests, learning, and behavioral needs. Further, differences among students in classrooms are not only to be tolerated but, in fact, encouraged. In addition, we claim that children differ at various grade levels, and that performance at subsequent grade levels is contingent, in large part, on exposures and experiences at preceding grade levels.

One can almost draw the inference that educators assume, because of the unbelievable progress made in science and math, that they know best what a child should learn, when he should learn it, and how he should go about learning it. Further, it appears that educators operate on the premise that not only do they know these things, they are the only ones who do. This position ignores the significance of learning which occurred before the child entered school, the intensity of his motivation to learn, and the frequency with which children, as they progress through the educational system, lose their desire to learn.

The school is concerned about developing communication skills, and it does this by insisting that children be quiet and not talk to one another.

Thus, we are not prepared to deal with problems we now face. (The question is, however, will our response to the current crisis be such that we will overlook or deemphasize programs which train persons to treat other crises which undoubtedly will arise?)

The apparent need for more engineers, mathematicians, and other scientific personnel contributed to the demand for more guidance counselors who were challenged to encourage students to enter colleges and universities. This contributed to the situation wherein more students sought admission to institutions of higher education and fewer elected to pursue programs of study necessary to gain technological competence. It appeared the only way to earn a ticket to the "good life" was through a college degree.

School populations were divided into two groups, those who would attend college and those who would not. Even though the latter group was larger in number, the bulk of educational dollars was expended to support programs for the former. This and other factors contributed to the present circumstances where there is a shortage of skilled labor, a surplus of persons who are without skills (potentially, there may be a time when there is a surplus of persons with academic training), and we appear to be approaching the time when it will be almost cheaper to purchase a new appliance than it is to have it repaired.

Certain other decisions have been made with respect to educational needs of selected groups. For example, when available, vocational subjects appear to be reserved for "slow learners," etc., and, intentionally or accidentally, are scheduled at times which conflict with academic courses. Pursuit of academic training thereby prevented a number of students from learning to use tools or master other basic vocational skills. At the same time, vocational courses seem to be held in low regard and are viewed as the domain of those who could not do anything else. The low priority given to vocational subjects in schools usually means that, in periods of financial crisis, these subjects are the last to be developed and the first to be eliminated. As a consequence students who, for a variety of reasons, do not elect to pursue further academic training, find there is nothing in school programs relevant to their needs or appropriate to their present circumstance. These students withdraw from school and seek employment in unskilled or semiskilled operations. Subsequent efforts to train them to enter skilled occupations are extremely expensive and, at this time, the efficiency of vocational training programs to meet job demands is questionable.

We have learned that the negative impact of environmental alterations can be reduced, provided the environment is permitted (in many cases, "treated") to approximate its original integrity. For example, pollution of streams, rivers, and lakes can be reduced, the use of various pesticides eliminated, game preserves established, new reefs created in oceans, and a variety of other conservation programs instituted.

Similar programs can be adopted for educational programs. That is, we can attempt to correct social environmental problems. If the poverty cycle is perpetrated because persons within the cycle have not been provided the skills, techniques, or hope they need if they are to escape, it seems reasonable for us to develop procedures whereby these needs are provided. We have, in fact, attempted to do this through the "war on poverty." (When this war is evaluated, we will probably find it to be the first war the United States has ever lost.)

Compensatory programs have been attempted, evaluated, and regarded as successful or unsuccessful—depending on the point of view of those who do the evaluation, and those who read the reports. Still, there seems to be an uneasy consensus among people that compensatory programs are not producing the results which are expected. Many reasons—"differences in intelligence levels among races," "compensatory programs are basically racist," "inadequate financial support"— have been advanced in order to explain the shortcomings of compensatory programs. Our concern is that most criticism overlooks the rationale, the structure, and the content of compensatory programs. It is almost as if the compensatory programs are felt to be appropriate, and that, therefore, the cause of failure must reside elsewhere.

It is evident, then, that when we attempt to explain shortcomings in compensatory programs, we use the same reasons we use when explaining the shortcomings in regular programs. This poses some interesting questions. Since, for the most part, students in compensatory programs are "homogeneous" with respect to economic backgrounds, is it possible that separation of "disadvantaged" children from "nondisadvantaged" children is an ineffective strategy? Or, is it possible that we are so locked into an academic orientation that we do not know how to evaluate programs? The answer to both of these must be "no." Otherwise, (1) we would not continue to pour money into programs specifically for disadvantaged children, and (2) "evaluation" would not be the "hottest buzz-word going."

We believe compensatory educational programs can serve to stimulate learning and meet behavioral needs if certain conditions are met: (1) The word "compensatory" should be dropped. This is essential in order to eliminate feelings that only children who are failing are assigned to these programs. (2) Teachers, administrators, and the community must analyze their own feelings in the matter. Regardless of name changes, etc., behavioral objectives—explicit and implicit, must be reviewed and expectancies—explicit and implicit, must be known. Without these analyses, program managers are apt to continue to maintain the position that, in the last analysis, the program is for persons who do not measure up. (3) The attitude that assignment to these programs must be reserved for a select group must be changed. (4) Curricula should be based on learning and behavioral needs of all students. (5) Divergencies in background experiences and needs must be accepted. (6) Procedures and strategies, rather than students, should be the subject of evaluation in order for the burden of proof to be shifted from children to program.

Our position in stating the above is to insist that compensatory educational programs have not produced the results which were hoped for because certain conclusions were drawn with respect to the impact of environmental circumstances of children, and it was implied that the only way to "improve their life styles" was through the rejection of "bad" environments. The problem with this is that a child's environment is real, whereas the reality of classroom programs is open to question.

We suggest the alternative is to eliminate judgments based on environmental circumstances, utilize real things students encounter in their lives as instructional devices, and grant students the right to make decisions concerning what they feel is appropriate and inappropriate to their personal lives.

The reader may question, then, the difference between compensatory education, as we discuss it, and the rest of the educational system. Our response is that there is no difference, and that the addition of "compensatory" education programs as separate and distinct units from "regular" educational programs indicates shortcomings in the total educational system which must be corrected. In our haste and intention to produce "well-educated people," we have ruled out a number of children. We must now institute steps to bring them back in, or else face the reality that whatever balance does exist in classrooms is in danger of being lost. By ignoring the individuality of children, and by subjecting them to the same set of standards, expectancies, and judgments, and then evaluating them, we have, in education, minimized certain environments. At the same time, we did not provide inhabitants of these environments with the skills they needed to cope with other environments.

If we are concerned with classroom ecology—as well we should be—we must adopt an educational position which is founded on an honest desire to utilize multiple teaching strategies appropriate to multiple standards. In such classrooms, all children—advantaged and disadvantaged, gifted and retarded, healthy and crippled—are inseparable parts of a whole. Thus, each child assumes an important role in the class because he is a child, not because he conforms to some classification system and not because he comes from a certain background.

In nature, there is an interaction among the different forms of animal and plant life. There is also interaction among children in schools and classrooms. Both interactions are modifiable as the result of environmental influences. The diversity of systems in nature leads to a common goal—namely, survival. The divergency which exists among children in schools and classrooms can also lead to a common goal—namely, an improved opportunity for learning and behavioral needs to be met.

We are certain every teacher and every administrator has heard at least once in his professional career that each child is a unique being. We expect that most teachers discover classrooms are composed of individual children presenting individual differences.

It is a pity we ignore what we see.

Instead of basing instructional patterns and strategies on what we know to be correct, we base them on the assumption that the class is a unit. Also, we assume children in the unit have as little interest in learning as we do. We fail to remember that at some point in the past we, too, were intensely interested in learning, but somewhere along the way we lost the urge; and we assist children to follow in our footsteps by treating them as we were treated.

Yet, there is optimism, with respect to the chances of a resurgence occurring in our own interest in learning, if we can make certain operational changes in teaching styles. If we change our notion of teaching from one where we do something to children to one which emphasizes that teaching is doing things with children, the response from the students may be such that we can see that learning can be fun rather than drudgery. When we say, "doing something with children," we do not refer to manipulation—rather, we refer to genuine involvement.

A child's desire to learn begins long before he enters school. Therefore, the school can nurture this desire, it can destroy this desire, but it does not create this desire.

It is possible more learning transpires around school buildings than inside them. Playground activities—particularly activities which develop spontaneously and are not under the supervision of teachers—contain many examples of learning. Play activities permit students to communicate with one another, to determine certain objectives, to define roles, to modify roles, and to develop many strategies and procedures appropriate to the attainment of objectives. On the playground, it is not unusual to find children who are in the process of discussing issues such as pollution, law enforcement, space and air travel, mechanics, automobiles, recreational plans, and many other things which are meaningful to them. It may be noisy, but learning is occurring. (Perhaps the noise level which accompanies this kind of learning situation is the largest detriment to its acceptance as an instructional technique. It appears schools and churches are the last bastions of silence in a noise-oriented society. Silence in churches indicates reverence. What does silence in schools represent?)

We mention silence, noise and playgrounds because they portray certain factors which should be considered when one deals with interaction among students. Noise undoubtedly is a concomitant of interaction, but there will also be periods of silence when students are busy in the execution of assignments which they feel are important. At times, the classroom should be a playground in that children will feel free to perform and test things out. Yet, at other times, it should resemble a church when children have the opportunity to observe the results of their efforts.

Outside the school there is interaction among students, and they learn from it. They may, in fact, learn much more than they do in typical classrooms. It seems plausible, then, that we should not be reluctant to carry the playground into schools. It may be noisy in schools if such interaction is permitted, but since when did silence become a virtue? After all, there is nothing more silent than the dead!

Since, regardless of efforts by adults to prevent it, children will relate to one another, it appears reasonable to include these relationships as integral parts of educational programs. If we accept this premise, we must also accept the corollary principle that the teacher's role must be changed in order to permit student participation in the entire spectrum of classroom activities—including planning.

Somehow, in the American educational system, we have come to the assumption that without adult domination, supervision and planning, children will become a group of savages. The authors suggest it is time for adults to examine the validity of the assumptions so willingly made.

The "generation gap," or the tendency by young people to react against the "establishment," should be reviewed by adults in the light of what adults have done to contribute to this gap or reaction. Society, as we know it, is becoming more and more an "establishment" in the eyes of young people and we, the older generation, are busy in the process of enlarging it. In our efforts to vicariously relive our youth through the lives of our children, we have introduced them into a highly structured society—much more structured than any society we encountered. For example, we have destroyed sandlot baseball. (To give full credit, we at least destroyed it in a sophisticated manner.) Apparently, we assume that because we as children had the freedom to make our own rules and determine our own procedures, we should specifically deny our own children this right. We have not been consistent, though, because today's school activities are based on the very things which happened to us when we were young and which we, for the most part, rejected. When it comes to schools, there is no generation gap if one compares the "favorite school periods" of adults, when they were children, with present-day children. It was as true then, as it is now, that the favorite period was, and still is, recess. This is strange when, for the most part we adults, as well as our children, could, and can, "hardly wait" to begin school. Easily, the first day of school is the most important day in people's lives. It is a tragedy that for us and, in turn, for our children, we learn that school is not all it is rumored to be. Nevertheless, children are still excited when they know they are almost eligible to enter school, and this excitement increases until the actual day of enrollment in school occurs.

When children go to school, they wish to go to school, they wish to enhance what they have already learned, and they wish to discover a world which is foreign to them. Why, then, is it that later, when we ask these youngsters what their favorite period is, their almost inevitable response is "recess"? The question, of course, is, can we convert educational programs to where recess periods are a continuation of learning experiences?

We believe we can. However, we believe this can only be done when we accept the reality that children demonstrate in their relationships with other children that they are capable of generating situations which contribute to their own learning. No doubt, some adult direction is needed. We believe, in fact, the role of the teacher is to serve as a monitor who provides the opportunity for children to discover efficient means whereby they can accomplish objectives they feel to be important. If the teacher really "gets with" his students, there is little doubts in our minds that the objectives children feel important will be at least equal to objectives determined by teachers.

All of this is characteristic of "progressive education." We realize the progressive movement in education is generally held in low repute by the educational system, and almost universally hated by school patrons. We realize also that, as a result, the "progressive education movement was scrubbed."

The problem, as we see it, is that the movement was eliminated for the wrong reasons. Student involvement was equated with license— in other words, let all the kids do their own things without any supervision or without introducing any accountability into the program. Teachers were not prepared to "manage" classrooms wherein students were given the opportunity to participate in planning what they were to do. As a consequence, teachers tended to withdraw from, rather than join in, classroom activities. This movement away from involvement is as ineffective as total domination, as far as providing learning opportunities is concerned. (Parenthetically, a major cry among adults is that children lack an awareness that they are accountable for their actions, or that they must, in a logical manner, defend their point of view. The question is, Where in a school program do we permit young people to become accountable for their own learning, or where do we provide the opportunity for them to learn to defend their positions?)

The point is that progressive education introduced an approach to meeting learning and behavioral needs. However, teacher preparatory programs did not provide the opportunity for inservice or prospective teachers to develop the skills which were necessary in order to maximize benefits which stem from student-teacher planning. Present teacher preparatory programs offer even less of a chance for a teacher to know how to relate to children because there seems to be an operational definition to the effect that a teacher is the summation of courses which he has completed during his college career. We believe this to be no more true than the behavioristic position in psychology which said, at one time, that the whole was equal to the sum of its parts.

Teacher preparatory programs must be changed if the full impact of the concept of classroom ecology is to be realized. This will be extremely difficult because, in the last analysis, teacher preparatory programs cut across the entire spectrum of academic offerings in a college or university. The quality of instruction has not been a significant issue in higher education, the relationship of general education courses to their avowed purposes (i.e., to produce well-educated people) is open to question, and there is a general reluctance in higher education to accept change. The burden of producing changes in teacher preparatory programs thus will fall on departments of education, and this certainly reduces the chances that any substantial changes will be made in the academic part of teacher preparatory programs. The possibility does exist, however, that education departments can implement programs which will enhance the ability of future teachers to relate to students.

The logical beginning point is in teacher training programs to give prospective teachers the opportunity to work with children beginning in the freshman year. Undergraduate students should be able to assume responsibility for determining their own training programs, if they have the opportunity to relate to children and plan joint educational programs with them. If beginning freshmen are given the opportunity to work with children, they can assume responsibility for planning a large part of their own educational programs. If this occurs (accepting the maxim that "teachers teach as they have been taught"), when these students become teachers they should be much more willing to permit children to plan learning situations than teachers who have not had such an opportunity.

Besides, early contact with children makes good sense from an economic standpoint. Before developing this point, let us consider that, at present, typical teacher training proceeds from an all-or-none point of view—the prospective teacher either completes the academic game mandated by certification requirements or he is not eligible to work in classrooms. This situation has produced results which are directly analagous to conditions in nature. For example, when the population of a species of animals exceeds the ability of the area to support them, the herd will suffer disease and a large number will die.

Schools suffer in a similar manner. The increased birthrate found us with an insufficient supply of both classrooms and teachers. Thus, the number of children exceeded our ability to handle them. We were able to improve the efficiency of construction of classrooms, but the improvement of teacher training and management policy is a different matter. Thus, under the rules of the game, we have crowded classrooms managed, in large part, by credentialled teachers who are almost forced to concentrate on the "bulk" of their students and ignore the "exceptions."

The accelerated costs of construction, the demand for increased pay by teachers, and the dissatisfaction of many school patrons have contributed in many areas to a "taxpayer revolt." So, in a time of inflated costs, school districts are encountering greater and greater resistance from those who must agree to "pay the bill." Schools are in the midst of a financial crisis, and this crisis will become worse unless alternative procedures are developed.

REASONING

We believe early experiences with children will enable us to develop alternative procedures for the following reasons:

1. We know a large number of freshmen students are forced—for

various reasons—to leave college before they complete degree requirements. Given the opportunity, many of these students can assume important roles in schools—particularly if we change our point of view
from individual classroom teachers to instructional teams. If freshmen students work with children—under the supervision of teacher
managers and college faculty members—they can become familiar
with school and classroom management procedures, as well as instructional principles. (In fact, the experiences students receive can be based
on particular interests and learning needs they exhibit.) Therefore,
students who withdraw from college prior to graduation will be qualified to enter various roles in schools. This differs from programs which
are designed to train paraprofessionals in that the program makes
"paraprofessional training" an integral part of the total teacher training process. More specifically, we feel paraprofessional training should
constitute one "rung" of a "career ladder" training program. Making
it a significant part of the teacher training process should result in an
increase in the scope of activities these persons undertake. The fact
that college students are being trained should permit the inclusion of
more contact with children. This, in turn, should enable teachers to
examine means whereby student interns can assume responsibility for
various facets of the instructional process.

2. The involvement of student interns provides a joint opportunity
for local schools and colleges to examine both teacher training procedures and concepts of the role of teachers in classroom management.
We need clarification of what a teacher is supposed to do, when he
should do it, and how it should be done, in light of the fact that our
present procedures are neither reducing class size nor enabling teachers
to cope with the spectrum of learning and behavioral needs which
exist in their classrooms. Hopefully, we will find it is possible to re-
structure the role of teachers, develop alternative educational strategies, and avoid the risk that the education system will price itself out
of existence.

3. The variety of experiences or activities student interns are given
can be ordered in such fashion that their involvement with children
progresses as competence increases. Note the emphasis on competence
rather than time. We see no reason to base what student interns do

on how they are classified in college (i.e., a student engages in activities because he is ready, not because he is a freshman, sophomore, etc.).

4. Student interns will have the opportunity to be actively involved with children, and this involvement should be beneficial to both. Also, it enables college faculty members to include an assessment of the student intern's ability to relate to children when faculty reach the point where they must judge whether or not students should be permitted to continue in teacher preparatory programs. This is vastly different from the present situation where the principal determinant for recommendation for a certificate is the quality of performance in academic courses. This also provides prospective teachers early in their college programs with an opportunity to decide whether or not they want to enter the teaching profession. The number of persons who complete teacher training programs, but who do not enter teaching, or who soon leave teaching, indicates the need for early decision-making.

5. Students will have the opportunity to move in and out of the teacher training process. In this manner they can pursue interests they may have, but which, under the present program, they must either ignore or delay.

6. College faculty members will have the opportunity to rediscover children and classrooms. This will be a traumatic experience to many, and this in itself indicates the need for the experience.

There are many advantages to student involvement with children. In the last analysis, though, we feel the most significant reason is that college students today really want to be involved. It will be a pity if we in education deny them this privilege.

CONCLUSION

In this chapter we have been concerned with education in general. We have said little about early childhood education because, unlike many, we do not believe early childhood education is an educational panacea. In fact, we believe the widespread interest in early education carries the inherent danger of even further fragmentation of educational procedures. For too long we have thought in terms of "elementary education" or "secondary education" or "higher education." In the process, we create gaps which must be "bridged," and we are uncertain as to how to go about it. The best technique seems to be to blame teachers at earlier grade levels for not having done their jobs properly.

We must begin to think in terms of education, and we must begin to realize that education is more than what happens in school. It is fortunate this is so because, based on what does happen in schools, it is easy to assume education provided by the school system in this country is critically ill.

Chapter 3

THE SCHOOL—PAST, PRESENT, AND FUTURE

ABOUT ONE HUNDRED YEARS AGO, the graded concept of elementary education became the traditional mode of school organization. From the initial adoption of this plan, educators recognized several vital shortcomings. In order to understand the traditional graded elementary organization, it is important to examine the graded school's historical background.

EVOLUTION OF THE TRADITIONAL SCHOOL

In the beginning, American education was not the unique and separate entity that it is today. Early education in the colonies transported its philosophies from the European countries from which the settlers had migrated. Europe had developed a rigid class system. Those children of the aristocratic class were given a classical education, while the children of the lower classes were expected to learn a trade through serving several years as an apprentice.

Because the colonists came from different European countries with different religious beliefs, languages, and customs, their educational philosophies naturally differed, and three somewhat dissimilar types of education emerged in the early colonies. These different types of educational philosophy were roughly grouped in the New England colonies (Massachusetts, Rhode Island, Connecticut, and New Hampshire), the Southern colonies (Virginia, Maryland, Georgia, North Carolina, and South Carolina), and the Middle Atlantic colonies (New York, New Jersey, Delaware, and Pennsylvania).

In 1642, in the New England colony of Massachusetts, the first school law was passed. This law compelled children to be instructed in certain laws, catechism, and to be taught a trade. This responsibility was left to the parents, and town officials were given the right to fine or jail parent, and demand apprenticeship for those who did not comply. The "Old Deluder Act" in 1647 required towns of fifty families to furnish an elementary school teacher, and towns of one hundred or more families to provide for a Latin grammar school, which was a tuition-supported college preparatory school for boys.

Sowards and Scobey (1961) suggest that the New England colonists had three motives for the interest in education: (1) religious—children had to be taught to read so they could learn the religious beliefs that New England colonies were founded upon; (2) political—children were to be taught the capital laws of the colonies; (3) economic—children had to become skilled workers so a large pauper class would not develop in the colonies as it had in Europe.

The education of young children was at this time carried on in dame schools. The dame was a woman who, in her home, taught children their ABC's and reading, thus preparing the boys for attendance in the town schools. The dame school education was usually all that the girls received.

The Southern colonies were far more socially stratified than New England. Formal education was thought to be a privilege of the upper class. Although there was some free public education, it was thought of as being charity and those who attended were considered paupers. Therefore, many people did not send their children to these schools because of the social stigma attached. The churches also had a strong influence on education and the educational goals were essentially the three previously mentioned for the New England colonies.

In the Middle Atlantic colonies during the 1600's, the population was sparse. This small population was made up of different religious groups and the schools were conducted by each local church parish.

During the 1700's, the churches still maintained control over most of the colonies' schools. The population continued to spread outward from towns in the New England area, and people in these outlying regions, because of distance and poor transportation, found it impossible to send their children to the town schools. Therefore, they succeeded in obtaining their own local schools separate from that in nearby towns, and these local schools became autonomous districts.

In the Middle Atlantic and Southern colonies, school development lagged behind that in New England. Although Thomas Jefferson advocated free public supported education, his plan was not accepted by many. In his Farewell Address of 1796, George Washington spoke of the importance of public education. These two prominent citizens, as did a few others, spoke out for the changes that were to occur in the next century.

According to Sowards and Scobey (1961), the United States had three main problems to solve during the 1800's before the development of the public elementary school could take place: (1) churches and schools had to be separated so our country could become united through democracy rather than religion; (2) control of the schools had to be reestablished at the state level, rather than in the local districts, so the state could assure all of the children an education; (3) education had to be supported by general taxation.

Sowards and Scobey state:

> The distinctive pattern of American public schools was truly taking form in the 1880's. The European system, a two-track affair as tended to perpetuate separate schools for upper and lower social classes, was rejected. The idea that everyone should go as far as his talents would permit was being accepted. The school system was increasingly tax-supported and secular in its control.
>
> Another essential ingredient to the realization of basic purposes was added through the idea of compulsory school attendance. The first law requiring school attendance was set down by Massachusetts in 1852, and most other states had taken a similar step by 1900. (Only the South lagged in this respect, since no Southern state had such a law on the books at that time.) The school, as we know it, was beginning to take shape.

Opening of the Quincy Grammar School by a man named John Philbrick set the pattern for more than one hundred years in American education. Although some attempts had been made prior to this time to establish a graded school organization, most of them had not been successful. Most of the previous instruction in American schools had been on an individual basis. The children merely memorized lessons and then recited them to their teacher. The textbooks used had not been uniform, many were of poor quality, and all were paid for by the parents. While one child was reciting his memorized lessons, the other children sat idly by, waiting their turn to recite. As classes became larger because of population expansion and migration to the cities, there were too many students per class for this type of organization.

The Quincy Grammar School, with its graded plan of organization, offered a solution to the problem by allowing one teacher to present lessons to a large group of students. The teacher utilized standard textbooks and instructed all of the students in the same subject matter. Thus, the traditional school evolved as a necessary type of organization, to enable the schools to provide an education for the ever-increasing number of elementary school children.

ORGANIZATION AND PHILOSOPHY OF TODAY'S TRADITIONAL SCHOOL

In the traditional school of today, admittance to grade one is compulsory at age six, with the birthdate to be on or before a certain date as prescribed by state law. Today, in America, many schools are conducted in the same manner, philosophically at least, as the Quincy Grammar School. After staying about nine months and completing a certain amount of work in the first grade, the child is passed on to the second grade, and then to the third, and so on annually from grade to grade until graduation, or until withdrawal from school. Instruction in this type of organization is carried out by utilizing graded texts, with every child in the class working approximately on the same page of the same text at the same time.

Holt (1968) sums up the philosophy of the traditional school in these three ways:

> (1) Of the vast body of human knowledge, there are certain bits and pieces that can be called essential—that everyone should know; (2) the extent to which a person can be considered educated, is qualified to live intelligently in today's world and be a useful member of society, depends on the amount of essential knowledge that he carries with him; (3) it is the duty of schools, therefore, to get this essential knowledge into the minds of children.

CRITICISM OF THE TRADITIONAL SCHOOL

The traditional school can be considered weak in several areas:

First, there is a lack of public-supported pre-elementary education. Children receiving instruction before entering first grade are usually those children whose parents can pay for private kindergarten or nursery school. These children are usually the children of parents in the middle class and above. Children of the lower socioeconomic level usually do not have the opportunity for pre-elementary instruction, and these children are the ones who are more likely to be lacking in experience and language development—two areas of learning that are necessary for success in school. The children from the rural depressed areas or from the inner city, the neglected children, or those of different language or cultural backgrounds, enter the first grade already far behind, and in the traditional school these minority children are destined, in most cases, to become failures even before they enter the first grade.

(It should be noted here that the term used in this chapter to denote the early education of children is "pre-elementary" rather than "preschool." "Preschool" is a misnomer. If a child attends school before entering elementary school, this education can be called "pre-elementary." However, if he is attending school, it is not accurate to say that he is attending "preschool.")

Second, first grade entrance for all normal children at the age of six is compulsory. Many children are not mature enough socially, emotionally, intellectually, or physiologically to do first grade work. Also, some children could successfully enter elementary school at age four or five. A strong public pre-elementary program would be a boon to helping place all children at a level where they could be successfully instructed by assuring that children would begin elementary school at the time when it would be most beneficial to them.

Third, reading instruction is begun at the same time for all elementary students. This is a weakness which should be corrected immediately. Reading begins before some are ready, and long after others are ready. The first year in elementary school may be the most critical time in a child's education. Many adjustments must be made upon school entrance. All educators recognize the fact that each child brings a different background of experiences with him. The traditional mode of mass instruction ignores this fact when all students begin reading at the same time.

Hoggard (1967) states: "One of the chief causes of reading failure is rushing children into the initial reading program before they are ready."

Recently Hoggard made a survey of seventy-two schools for the purpose of discovering practices regarding reading readiness. It was alarming to find that twenty-seven schools started all first graders in the preprimer during the first or second week in school. It was more alarming to learn that four school systems started all first graders in the primer. The explanation was made by the schools that since the primer contains all the vocabulary to be found in the preprimer, the program simply starts with the primer in order to save time.

Hoggard goes on to state that parents and teachers expect all children to begin reading shortly after school begins in September. Some children cannot at this time adequately learn to read. The pressure on them makes the task of learning to read become distasteful and creates anxieties about reading.

A fourth major weakness of the traditional school is mass class instruction and memorization of text material. Little regard is given to the child's native ability, his interests, or his past experiences. Critical thinking skills are not developed—rather, memorizing facts from the textbooks is emphasized. The use of patterns, identical assignments, and allowing no deviations from the group standards is detrimental to creativity.

A serious inadequacy is seen when students read at the correct instructional level—the level where the child can successfully perform. The fallacy of this procedure can be seen by examining reading instruction. Bond and Tinker (1967) point out the importance of reading by stating: "Reading is generally recognized to be the most important subject taught in the elementary school. Proficient reading is essential as a tool for learning a large portion of subject matter throughout successive school levels."

In most schools all children are expected to read the basal text for their grade level. Bond and Tinker write that 15 to 20 percent of the school pupils are severely retarded in reading. Yet, Hoggard (1967) says that most reading difficulties in the schools can be prevented, with the exception of about 5 percent. This high percentage of "failures" has been caused by mass teaching of all children in the class. Failure of retardation in reading can be the cause of disabilities in other curriculum areas since reading is a vital tool of learning.

A fifth major traditional school weakness is regimented discipline and insistence of compliance with restrictive standards—a weakness fostered and perpetuated by school administrators and teachers, and tolerated by parents. Teachers say that this is a necessity in order to manage or control a large group of children in the traditional classroom.

A sixth major weakness is the utilization of an annual lock-step promotion or retention policy. Children who can do the prescribed work are promoted annually to the next grade. Children who cannot do the work are either retained in a grade or given a social promotion. Retention in a grade has always been equated with failure and many children carry the stigma of failure with them throughout their lives because of this traditional school policy. The children who are capable of learning more material than the prescribed amount are still compelled to move along at the same pace as their classmates, and cover the same material. They are seldom allowed to move ahead or work independently.

All of the above points criticizing the traditional school or organization and philosophy can be summed up as follows:

The traditional school does not consider the child as an individual. His own social, emotional, and educational needs are not considered, and he is a member of a grade and class which does not provide for, or recognize him as being, a unique human being.

THE TRADITIONAL SCHOOL AND INDIVIDUAL DIFFERENCES

People are different. This is not a new idea, and if one takes the time to look around him, simple observation will support this statement. Children in learning situations are also different because they are individuals. Richey (1968) writes that the fact people are different is not so startling, but what is startling is the extent of the differences.

Experimentation during the latter part of the nineteenth century led to discovering the many ways that children differ. The amount of variance discovered indicated that groups of people possessed chracteristics which fell into a curve of normal distribution. No longer could a teacher classify her entire class as fast, dull, average, etc.

The children in any group will have a wide range of abilities, achievement, attitudes, and physiological characteristics. On the basis of this fact, no teacher can make uniform assignments and expect every child in her group to achieve the same amount of learning as every other child in the group.

No teacher can make the same assignment of homework and expect to challenge all the children. In fact, there is good reason to doubt that homework has any positive value except to pacify parents who expect it because they were given homework while attending a traditional school.

Many parents and teachers do consider individual differences. According to Goodlad (1966), they do not consider the whole spectrum of human variability but have a more narrow concept of differences. They think of a particular child in relation to the traditional school curriculum which contains a rigid and narrow set of subject matter. Thus, they consider how well the child performs the scope of the subject matter within his grade. To them, this is the concept of individual differences.

This narrow view of individual differences held by parents and teachers is reflected in traditional school practices. Goodlad cites, as an example, that while supposedly considering individual differences and differentiating instruction, poorer readers of one grade, at the end of the school year, may be receiving reading instruction from the same basal text that the more skilled readers used at the beginning of the year, showing that the teacher thinks the range of differences in reading is only one grade level. In many cases, when the teacher seeks to differentiate reading instruction by placing the child on his own reading level—the instructional level—for reading instruction from a basal reading text below his grade in school, parents complain that the child is not in the right book. Reading below grade level is considered by the parents to be a sign of failure. The classic illustration of this view is found in the statement, "Whoever heard of a fifth grader not reading from a fifth grade text?"

Goodlad reports on a study he conducted concerning academic variability among fourth graders. The population sample consisted of over ten thousand parents and teachers in eleven states. He defines a fourth grader as "a child enrolled in the fourth grade who scores between 4.0 and 4.9 on a standardized achievement test taken at mid-term (January)." The question that Goodlad elicited responses to was, "What percentage of a fourth grade class is at grade level?"

An answer was selected from these responses: less than 20 percent; 20 to 40 percent; 40 to 60 percent; 60 to 80 percent; 80 to 100 percent. The first selection is the correct response. The answers of the parents and teachers, however, fell into the pattern of a bell-shaped curve peaking slightly to the left of center, and Goodlad comments on these results by writing, "Obviously there is much to do in merely teaching the facts of individual differences to persons who deal with individuals every day."

Researchers know that although teachers, parents, and school administrators possess knowledge, they may not necessarily use it. Educators have for many years been speaking of individual differences. Either they understand the concept and do not use this knowledge, or they do not actually grasp the idea. There is reason to believe that many teachers in the graded school actually do not understand what is meant by the concept of individual differences, and that colleges engaging in the training of teachers are not developing this understanding in potential teachers.

It is also possible that colleges are preparing potential teachers in the area of individual differences, but that it is easier for the teachers not to take care of the differences once they reach the classroom.

A good example is the standardized group tests which are designed for group measurement, but often are misused as an individual assessment. Most teachers look at the individual's achievement, yet fail to look at the distribution of scores of the entire class.

Educators should be aware of the following points when planning for the instruction of different children in the same classroom:

1. The spread of ability increases as children progress to higher grades. In other words, in the sixth grade, the spread of ability will be greater than in the first or second grade.

2. In subject areas such as arithmetic, where there is little opportunity for children to learn outside of school, the spread of ability is generally not any greater than the mental age of the child. Very few children study arithmetic independently. However, in subjects such as the language arts, where the child can readily have access to supplementary materials to facilitate independent learning, the spread may be one or two times the number of the grade level.

The above statements indicate that if children had access to individualized instruction in all subject areas, they would have a greater range of achievement.

Children make irregular progress in different subject matter areas. For example, a fifth grade student may achieve the sixth grade level (such as grade 6.4) in spelling, the fifth grade level in science (say, 5.9) and social studies (say, 5.2), and the fourth grade level in math (say, 4.8) and reading (say, 4.6). This particular child would be said to have a range of 1.8 grades. Some students vary much more than this in the range of different subject matter area scores. Some children who are considered normal by teachers and peers range as much as two to two-and-one-half years in subject matter areas.

Very few children in a grade actually achieve in all subject areas at their expected level. Probably in today's heterogenous-grouped classroom, only three or four fourth graders actually attain at the middle of the school year (January) the 4.0 to 4.9 range in all subject areas.

Learning of certain subject matter is considered by many people the goal of education, and the graded school is the instrument of teaching this subject matter. We all know that if a student does not learn the required material for a grade, he will be retained. Supposedly, he will learn the material the next year. In this way, the traditional school makes the students fit the grade level standards. However, research has shown that retention does not cause students to learn the required subject matter, nor has this practice reduced the range of achievement within each grade—but this practice still continues. These research findings have been published for many years, and one wonders why teachers and administrators have failed to take heed.

Many schools still practice nonpromotion for the child who does not measure up to the year's standard of work. Many parents believe that if a child has not mastered the material of one level, he cannot be passed on through the hierarchy of the graded school regardless of what we know to the contrary.

Research indicates that the nonpromotion practice seriously injures the child's self-image and hurts his social adjustment. Knowing this and the fact that the child does no better the second year in a grade, why do we continue this practice?

In many cases, teachers give the grade of F to a child who cannot measure up to a prescribed standard because of low intelligence. This is analagous to shooting all men and women who cannot fly by flapping their arms.

OXYMORA OF EDUCATION

An oxymoron is a combination, for epigrammatic effect, of contradictory or incongruous words ("cruel kindness," "sweet sorrow," "I love you to death"). For years in education we have been espousing the virture of testing and labeling children. The label seems to stick throughout the child's school career, and every teacher who sees the label tends to assign that same label to the child. In other words, if we say the child is retarded in the first grade, this is passed on to the second grade teacher and she treats him as a retarded child. If we say the child is gifted in the first grade, this is passed on to the second grade teacher and she assigns him good grades. Research has indicated that when researchers tell teachers that children in a certain group will be late bloomers, and other children will "wither," then this prophesy becomes a reality.

Today, educators and psychologists are saying, "Let's test the children earlier than ever before. Let's test them at the age of three or four." This is oxymoronic. Rather than treating a symptom that is depriving the child of an opportunity to be educated—to learn with children his own age, we are now saying, "Let's label the child at the age of three, and this label will then become a self-fulfilling prophesy." The very moment this child is labeled, he is no longer able to compete with other children in the same classroom. The children from the upper socioeconomic levels, and particularly from the upper middle class, are always getting the good labels, and really have very little trouble in school. The children who get the bad or derogatory labels generally come from the disadvantaged areas and are branded as being nonproducers before they even start to school.

Naturally, another oxymoron of education has already been mentioned earlier in this chapter and that is we as educators say, "Let's take care of individual differences," and then we immediately give every child the same textbook in the first grade, second grade, and so on.

There are many oxymora in education, but probably one of the most devasting to the young child from the disadvantaged area, minority group, or broken home, is the "self-fulfilling prophesy" oxymoronic prediction. This prophesy is as devastating as a bullet to the brain.

A COLLEGE TRAINING PROGRAM

There is, among educational researchers, a widespread acceptance of the rather trite expression, "Teachers teach as they have been taught." It follows that teachers are not likely to be able to individualize instruction unless they have had the opportunity to participate in a program in which their own instruction has been individualized.

Teachers are not likely to provide children with options, or accept the fact that responsibility for learning resides in the learner, unless they have had options and have accepted the responsibility for their own learning. It is not possible for them to develop variable educational strategies which reflect individual needs unless they have participated in a program which utilizes variable strategies based on individual progress and individual needs. They cannot be expected to reverse the procedures which emphasize diagnosis, analysis, and assessment of children to the diagnosis, analysis, and assessment of educational strategies unless they have had the opportunity to select strategies, analyze the expectancies of these strategies, and assess the efficiency of the strategies to meet the individual priorities and objectives which children have established.

THE NEW SCHOOL

The new school must begin when the child is very young. Age four is an ideal time to begin readiness for most children. We must be cognizant, however, that schools should ask the question, "What's the child ready for?" and not give all children the same readiness material.

A new direction does not necessarily call for a complete revolution in pre-elementary practices. Determination of a new direction should flow from an analysis of what is known about good educational practices and knowledge of the child in a modern society. This direction calls upon the tradition of the pioneers of the pre-elementary school whose message should still be heard today:

The kindergarten will grow in value as our vision of life and our insight into the meaning of education deepen and broaden. It will be altered from year to year by reflection upon what we have attempted and what we have accomplished. Out of this will come a new vision, a higher standard which will enable us to reconstruct and create newer and more ideal courses of study for the children of the future. (Hill, 1913).

In the next ten years, Shane and Shane (1969) indicate that education will reverse its traditional pattern of expenditures. Major support for early childhood education seems very probable, and a reduction in expenditure is evident in secondary education.

They also indicate that educators will assume a formal responsibility for children when they reach the age of two. This writer thinks, though, that age two is too early for educators to assume a formal responsibility.

Shane and Shane also envision that the new programs for two-year-olds will involve the coordination of community resources which will be supervised under the auspices of the school, and will equalize educational opportunities for certain children before cultural deprivation makes inroads on their social and mental health.

The article by Shane and Shane, which is a prediction of these two people for schools in America in the 1970's, envisions the minischool which will provide a program of carefully designed experiences for the three-year-old. These experiences will be deliberately devised to increase the sensory input from which the children derive their intelligence. Each minischool will enroll six or eight children under a qualified paraprofessional. This paraprofessional will be prepared in childhood environmental experiences and will supervise clusters of approximately six minischools.

In all probability, these small schools will be built in housing projects or as part of new schoolhouses, or in individual self-contained buildings.

This excellent article further states that the pre-primary continuum is a new creation intended to replace contemporary kindergartens for the four-and five-year-olds. This program assumes that the young learner will spend from one year to four years preparing himself to perform in a primary continuum which is the segment of education now labelled grades one through three. They state that the pre-primary interval should sharply reduce the problems of widely varied experiences and social adjustment encountered by children who are enrolled in the first grade at age six, regardless of their previous experiences.

From the same article by Shane and Shane, we find that the environmental mediation for two-to six-year-olds, as described above, will permit schools to abandon the current concept of nongrading. Instead, we will have a continuum of coordinated learning experiences from about age two through secondary schools.

There is one point in the article with which this writer disagrees. It is stated that promotion problems will also vanish, since in such a continuum of learning there are no specific points at which a student passes or fails. It is further stated that the student merely moves ahead at his own pace, and that grade cards are likely destined to disappear.

It should be pointed out that for one hundred years or more in American schools, educators with foresight and creativity have tried to eliminate the problems of promotion, but have had little success. People tend to want grades for their children, and teachers tend to give grades to the children. This is a sticky problem that can only be dealt with through a mass American program where all schools go to a no-grade system. That would be very difficult to accomplish but could be done and, of course, should be done.

It must be pointed out that when we speak of progressive education in America in the 1970's, there are still places in this country where educational programs appear as they did one hundred years ago. In the Appalachian Mountains there are several thousand one-or two-room schools which are warmed by pot-bellied wood-burning stoves and have outdoor toilets. Most of the children look forward to "getting on welfare" when they grow up.

Of the children in Perry County, Kentucky, who started to school in 1948, only 12 percent finished the twelfth grade—and this was America in 1969.

If the changes mentioned by Shane and Shane take place, then we can expect that in the mid-1980's, students will probably graduate from high school with knowledge and social insight equal or superior to that of a person who earned a bachelor's degree in 1969.

If the child has had the benefit of carefully developed learning opportunities in a skillfully mediated milieu since he was two or three years of age, then we can expect colleges to offer advanced courses to these students, when they reach the freshman level, that we now offer our graduate students.

Also, it is highly likely that in the 1980's we will have media specialists for elementary schools, and culture analysts for elementary, intermediate, and high schools to consult with teachers concerning our growing insights into how an inferior culture shapes the learning and behavior of its children. There is a good possibility that special education will not be necessary because the children from disadvantaged backgrounds will have been receiving educational opportunities since the age of two, and the handicapped children remaining in our society will be cared for in the regular classrooms. All of these things can be expected to come about by 1990.

By the turn of the century, the basal series will be much more interesting than educators ever dreamed. Because the child will have been exposed to so much, from the age of two until he is ready for the basal series, he will be able to read at a much higher level. Therefore, he will be reading interesting things such as honeymoons on the moon, a weekend in space, a trip to various planets, or a voyage around the earth via a spacecraft. All of these topics will be read by the six-year-old who will have a reading vocabulary of two or three thousand words.

Although it is anticipated that these events will come about in the progressive school systems throughout this country, let us hope that we do not have left in America, at the turn of the century, any schools having pot-bellied stoves for heat, or outdoor toilets. Let us also hope that we lead the world in literacy.

REFERENCES

Bond, G. L., and Tinker, M. A.: *Reading Difficulties.* New York, Appleton-Century-Crofts, 1967.

De Young, C. A., and Wynn, R.: *American Education.* New York, McGraw-Hill, 1968.

Goodlad, J. I.: *School Curriculum and the Individual.* Waltham, Mass., Blaisdell, 1966.

Hill, Patty Smith: Second report. *The Kindergarten.* Boston, Houghton Mifflin, 1913, pp. 274-275.

Hillson, M.: *Change and Innovation in Elementary School Organization.* New York, Holt, Rinehart and Winston, 1965.

Hoggard, J. K.: Readiness is the best prevention. In Harris, A. J. (Ed.): *Readings on Reading Instruction.* New York, David McKay, 1967.

Holt, J.: *How Children Fail.* New York, Pitman, 1968.

Richey, R. W.: *Planning for Teaching.* New York, David McKay, 1967.

Sowards, G. W., and Scobey, M. M.: *The Changing Curriculum and the Elementary Teacher.* San Francisco, Wadsworth, 1961.

Thomas, G. I., and Crescimbeni, J.: *Individualizing Instruction in the Elementary School.* New York, Random House, 1967.

Chapter 4

READINESS

THE DEFINITION OF readiness has almost as many facets as people who try to define it. As Keliher (1967) implies, readiness begins at birth and ends only with death. It is a lifetime matter. As a matter of fact, some theologians believe our whole natural life is merely a readiness period for life after death.

In the early part of this century, according to Davis (1963), E. L. Thorndike reported three identifiable laws of learning. They were the laws of (1) readiness, (2) exercise, and (3) effect.

The law of readiness states that when any conduction unit is in a state of being ready, it is satisfying for it to act, and annoying not to act. Many interpretations of the above description of readiness have tended to blur the operational definition. In the operational sense, readiness is thought of as being "composed of various cyclical acts and intellectual functions that have, as a common goal, the acquisition of a definite behavior or knowledge.

The term "readiness" as applied to pre-elementary school education has many connotations. What is the child ready for? The reply depends on past experiences of the person who answers. Each sees the term in the light of his own interests and viewpoint. Each has his own ideas of the principles around which pre-elementary school education should be centered. Each has an idea of the curricula to be followed in the education of the young child.

READINESS FROM THE ACADEMIC VIEWPOINT

There are those who think of a child as a little adult, and these people generally impose readiness from an academic viewpoint. These individuals look upon the college years as a period in which the individual gets ready for his "industrial life." High school, naturally, is a readiness period for college. For the academically oriented people, elementary school time is a period when readiness for high school is drilled into youngsters, and the pre-elementary school years are the days when a child must be molded into a neat little form which will best enable him to get a good start in first grade.

Some are even more narrow in their outlook. To them, readiness means only reading readiness or language arts readiness. Reading, in their estimation, is the process of getting information from printed material; therefore, readiness comes in books, and a child is made "ripe" by being shown how to do the exercises in workbooks which really are generally "watered-down" pre-primers. Later, if he does not give the correct responses in the tool subjects, he is a failure.

THE REAL FAILURE

Who really fails, though? Parents fail their children when they allow them to be denied—when they substitute for healthy play and experiences a prescribed, formalized, routinized schedule of activities designed to produce robots that give correct answers.

When we think of readiness in its relation to subject matter, there is a result of limited interpretation. When planning an activity program, observing a child's adjustment, recognizing individual differences, and in measuring total progress of every child and also that of the group, all teachers must consider the many aspects of readiness.

Many educators know that readiness and the subject matter areas have a close relationship, and also know that children will show an obvious sign when they are ready to begin reading, writing, spelling, and arithmetic. If a teacher fails to observe the signs, the child is the one who suffers. He may be pushed too hard and fast in a particular tool area. The teacher particularly faces a dilemma when a child indicates readiness for one aspect of learning, but not another which is supposed to be taught at the same time. He should be given instruction only in the area for which he is ready.

Some of the signs for which the teacher looks are the ability to sit still and keep the eyes fixed on reading material, to listen to and follow directions, and to keep the eyes fixed on the reading material for the required length of time. Other signs are the capacity to gather meanings from context, to remember word forms, to reason, to anticipate, and to form meaningful associations.

PHYSIOLOGICAL, PSYCHOLOGICAL, AND SOCIAL ASPECTS OF READINESS

Most authorities who have studied children in the pre-elementary school years agree that this period is the most important time for developing readiness for both short-range and long-range activities in and out of the formal school. Many think of readiness as particularly associated with their own field of study and have worked out programs to remediate flaws in a child's development.

Some authorities even go so far as to say that a child learns seventy-five percent of all he ever learns by the age of six.

Getman (1966) stresses the organismic basis of learning. He states that visual learning is responsible for approximately 80 percent of our acquired knowledge, and that when dealing with symbols and forms, the child must be able to perceive them correctly and interpret them adequately. He also feels that the perception of symbols is highly related to physiological development and has added a new dimension to the assessment of readiness. He stresses perceptual readiness and has organized an action program to develop it.

The theory of sensory-motor activities helping to develop readiness is held by many modern-day observers of the pre-elementary school or early education-oriented child. This theory is not new because Piaget first explained the role of sensory-motor activity in the baby's early learning. Piaget pointed out that the child looks and listens, and feels with his hands the things around him. He combined the tactile, auditory, and visual perceptions which, according to Piaget, produce structures in the mind which can be used in thinking. This basic sensory-motor learning continues throughout life and is extremely important during the pre-elementary school years. For example, as a child climbs a ladder, he not only develops skill in controlling his body movements, but also learns to estimate distances and develops a sense of balance.

SENSORY DEVELOPMENT

As a child dances to music and simulates an Indian rain dance, he is developing his auditory, visual, and kinesthetic experiences. When the young child learns to put together ideas concerning what he has seen, heard, and felt, he is using his perceptual-motor learning to develop readiness. He learns because he is having meaningful experiences. He is laying a foundation on which to build. Unfortunately, many children have limited experiences.

TEACHER OBSERVATION

One outstanding feature of the early learning years is the quality and amount of growth made in such a short time. The child's bones and muscles grow rapidly while his height and weight increase simultaneously. The teacher should note not only the growth, but the child's awareness and understanding of everything around him, because these things indicate how well he is getting ready for more experiences.

The growth, motor readiness, and reading readiness should be judged in the same way. The motor skills on which reading, writing, and arithmetic depend, are subject to the same physiological growth which governs creeping, walking, and grasping. As a child falls down in his early efforts to stand and walk, he may also fall down in the motor aspect of his learning efforts. He may be ready, but cannot get control all at once.

VISION

Vision appears to play an important part in the growth of readiness. Opthamologists tell us that the development of vision in each child is very complex and goes through countless stages of evolution to bring vision to an advanced state. Vision is as intricate in its development as speech or reading, and all three must be ready to work with the child in full control before he can be said to be in a state of readiness for reading, writing, and arithmetic.

SELF-IMAGE

A very important phase of early education which leads to a state of readiness in the children is the development of an adequate self-image. A child who unconsciously thinks, "I like me," has developed a positive self-image and is ready to function in social situations. A child does not live in a vacuum in our modern world, and a person must have a positive self-image to be able to take his part in our social life. A child who can find pleasure in relationships with his peers, with his teachers, and other adults has developed a readiness for social living. In some children this must be developed during the pre-elementary school years.

READINESS OF THE WHOLE CHILD

It is almost trite to say that, when we think of readiness, we should consider all aspects of the child. However, it is true. We speak in terms of mental, physical, social, and emotional growth, but it is the entire child who goes to school, the entire child who succeeds or fails. We recognize that he may be ready for some things while not ready for others. But, too often, we try to treat the symptoms of the "things" and forget about Johnny, Sally, or Bill.

Davis (1963) says that acquiring readiness, like all learning, should be looked upon as a springlike developmental pattern and not as various items, content, or experiences occurring at predetermined times. Every preparatory experience should travel toward a goal, and at the same time push back to the first experience that forms the base. Each systematic stage of readiness is a step toward the next stage, and all stages overlap.

Any teacher will tell us that within a given age group there is a wide range of abilities and differences in various areas. This is particularly true concerning children in the pre-elementary school group where a difference of six months in chronological age may mean many more months difference in readiness. The sex of the child may also cause a variation in relation to readiness. Boys, as a rule, are slower than girls to reach readiness for school subjects, but they are ahead in motor development. Many authorities say that boys should begin first grade at age seven, while girls should begin at age six.

Readiness, like ability, is a highly personal matter. The child should be his own motivator. At a point in time, he will be "ripe." That is to say, he will be if he is not hampered by a great number of restrictions placed on him by parents and adults who think they will make him ready. It seems unimportant to parents that it is not necessarily his way of developing. Children will develop at their own speed and in their own way with a great deal of efficiency, if adults realize this, and the child will be the better for it. Some parents rush and push their children too much. They do not let the children enjoy being children.

PRESSURES

The pressure to achieve more often than not constricts rather than expands. The child is rushed from one experience to another so fast that he has no time to get ready for the next step. In our fast-moving and modern society, children often have little time for contemplation and quiet moments. First-hand experiences that the child would enjoy when he gets ready for them are many times eliminated as the readiness-conscious parent prepares one experience after another for him. The word "hurry" has become addictive. Emphasis is placed on how many things a child does, how fast he does them, and how many books he has read—not on how well he enjoys them.

DIFFERENCES

Individual differences are evident, if one knows what to look for, and should be considered first. A child's personal growth curve gives a good indication of his readiness for school subjects. The child who grows slowly may not be "ready" at the age of six to enter first grade, but that does not mean he will not attain the same level of achievement at a later date.

LEARNING

We agree that all children do not learn in the same way. A child may not be ready to function in an accepted way, but he may achieve in a manner peculiar to him. If he is continually thwarted and made to do everything to fit a pattern which is foreign to his nature, he may give up the struggle and regress to a state of permanent unreadiness. He may also lose whatever creative ability he possesses. This is often the fault of the school and the teacher. It is also the fault of parents.

New experiences provide their share in building confidence and security in a child, if the adult in charge knows and accepts the child's level of readiness for each new experience. If this is not taken into account, and if the experience is something with which the child is not ready to cope, it may fill him with a fear that can never be completely erased—or it may cause him to dislike something or someone that would have been a pleasure to him later when he is ready.

Common experiences must be as carefully handled as new experiences. Life's daily events often pile up feelings and set patterns in such a way that emotional upsets occur. If the child is to be secure and feel adequate, now and in the future, most of his experiences must be chosen by him.

The question then arises as to how many things must be postponed until the child is ready. Naturally, some learnings cannot be postponed. Health and safety precautions, for example, must be taught—but on a level which the child can understand.

Learning and readiness for learning have a better chance of success in an environment which allows the child the use of his five senses to build bridges from the concrete to the abstract. If the experiences fit together in order that he can see the connections, he can build them into a structure that is meaningful. The building takes place while he manipulates objects, asks questions and solves problems either partially or in whole, and also while he plays and creates new things. Readiness thrives best in an environment which primes the child to ask questions and search for the best solutions.

A child in a pre-elementary school class can easily be helped to develop reading readiness. He has many, many opportunities for speaking and listening. He reads when he goes to a crayon box that is labeled, or sees the charts, labels, lists, and names in the room. He is building readiness when he enjoys the coloring books; when the teacher reads a story; when the children, with the teacher's help, write a story about an experience.

Olson (1949) set up five stages (using language arts to illustrate his point) with which to measure the progress of children: (1) The child has acquired direct sensory experiences of feeling, smelling, tasting, seeing, and hearing. (2) The child can understand and follow the simple speech of others—that is, he can comprehend. (3) The child can differentiate his own speech sounds so he can talk with others. (4) When a child enters first grade, he has a large command of oral language and functional grammar, and has learned that there is a connection between experience and oral language, and between pictures, words, and experiences. In this fourth stage he is able to read when he learns the relationship between systematically arranged symbols, experience and oral language. (5) The child, through writing and associated spelling, gains power of communication.

According to Olson's research, parents and teachers were not able to hasten the child's progress through these stages. When he checked the records of those children who appeared to learn to read "spontaneously" in the pre-elementary school or at home, he found they tended to be rapid growers who were in the fourth stage.

Children who were not making much progress in the second and third grades he found were slow growers just entering the fourth stage. A variability as great as this is to be expected among children, but many people find it hard to accept the idea that during this stage of readiness they should pace the child instead of forcing him.

In pre-elementary school education in America, too much emphasis is often placed on standardized testing, evaluation, curricula, textbooks and workbooks. This results in a great amount of classification and regimentation. This does not serve the needs of children who do not fit the norm. Some resist for a time, but eventually surrender. Others surrender meekly without a protest. A few creative ones—the artists and the rebels—continue to struggle. They want to express their own reactions to life. They will not surrender readily or submit easily to becoming "a right-answer person." Children need freedom to be different. They need freedom in order to express feelings of anger, aggression, frustration, sadness, sorrow, pleasure, and joy in ways not destructive to self or others. Too many adults mistrust children and will not allow them freedom, and insist that they be small adults.

Some adults do not wish to face the honest challenges of four- and five-year-olds. But how can a child develop readiness for the many things which will later confront him when he is constantly made to conform to a pattern—made to fit the mold.

In our society adults impose too many formal evaluation techniques on children. Also, they rigidly structure the environment for children offering them bribes for conformity, instead of for originality. Such exercises may give statisfaction to adults, but they do little for children.

Too often, teachers do not respect the creativity in children. The child is too often assigned many forms to be colored and many patterns to be traced. They are drilled unmercifully, and they must practice and practice. The teachers give too much seat work having little to do with anything useful. Very often this seat work is just to keep the child quiet. Again, in the school as well as at home, we reward children for "right answers."

In a good pre-elementary school situation child, teachers, and parents can work and learn together. The child can teach his little brothers and sisters as he is learning in the preschool years. The parents can engage in the children's activities, and they can learn together. The teacher can work with the parents, thereby helping the children. Creativity can be stressed and rewarded. It would be good for parents and teachers to forget for a few hours each the "right answer syndrome."

Parents should be aware, too, of readiness. Very often the parent is frustrated if the child does not do something when the parent thinks it is time, not realizing that maturation has not taken place. When the parent puts too much pressure on the child at such a time, then only frustration and maladjustment can occur. This is as bad as the "right answer syndrome."

There is quite a difference between readiness among children at the same age level, as well as among children at different age levels. Because this is true, it becomes essential that each child be given a chance to use the material and activities which are most interesting to him at a specific time.

Children who are the same age should not be expected by adults to take part in the same play activity as the majority just because they are the same age. They should be free to play individually if they wish at the pre-elementary school and at home. However, occasionally, if a child is withdrawn or if the teachers and parents suspect maladjustment, then the activities for this child should be structured for his own good. Along these lines, too, the parents and teachers must be aware of what is going on, and be alert in order to prevent marked abnormal tendencies from developing in the child.

Recognizing and cooperating with children's readiness is necessary in every area of learning because building on children's spontaneous interest is the essence of good teaching and generally brings excellent results.

If the child does not receive guidance and encouragement at the pre-elementary age, then the learning process may be impeded. Providing richly for the blooming capacities of the rapidly growing children in the pre-elementary school is a basic responsibility of all the adults concerned. Putting off providing for them on the basis that the children are too young is poor reasoning and will produce poor results.

Taylor (1967) tells us that they may be brilliant later, but never again will children learn and develop as fast in any five-year stretch as in the first years of their lives. In this very short span, a baby, starting with only the basic equipment for learning, becomes a person in his own right. Because there are no previous experiences to color them, a baby's first impressions are deep, clear, and lasting. Often the child has built a group of traits, attitudes, and emotional responses which forms his unique personality and determines his characteristic reactions for life before his parents are aware of what is happening.

Spontaneity, self-choice, fantasy, intelligence, and vigor cannot be minimized in planning an environment conductive to readiness.

Readiness to increase the vocabulary becomes apparent when the child begins to play. He needs words to define and explain new play-experiences. Words help actions become symbolic representations.

A child needs physical as well as mental work in order to tackle his challenging environment. He needs a coordinated body with considerable motor skills to explore space, determine directions, elevations, and distances, and to become knowledgeable concerning the outer world.

There is no reliving the age of pre-elementary school. It is a powerful age for learning. It is a spontaneous, self-motivating age in which active sensory processes are operating every waking hour of the day. It is the golden age of readiness. It is the "teachable time" for most children.

REFERENCES

Davis, D. C.: *Patterns of Primary Education.* New York, Harper and Row, 1963.

Getman, G. N., and Kane, E. R.: *The Physiology of Readiness.* Minneapolis, PASS, 1966.

Keliher, A. V.: Many dimensions of readiness. *Childhood Education, 43*: 442-443, 1967.

Olson, W. C.: *Child Development.* Boston, Heath, 1949.

Taylor, K. W.: *Parents and Children Learn Together.* New York, Teachers College Press, 1967.

Chapter 5

TECHNIQUES FOR TEACHING MATHEMATICS TO PRESCHOOL CHILDREN

Most preschool children must be treated with caution when we introduce arithmetic concepts because many of these children have very limited background experiences. In fact, experiences the teacher takes for granted in children from middle or upper class environments may be quite unknown to the disadvantaged child. Therefore, teachers must provide suitable experiences for some children before concepts based on these experiences are introduced (i.e., concepts should be presented in a concrete rather than abstract manner). This dictates that the introduction of a new topic must proceed from everyday use and concrete level to a semiconcrete level, and from there to an abstract level.

The primary purpose for instruction in arithmetic is to enable the child to recognize and cope with mathematical problems found in daily life. Since many mathematical concepts are abstract, these skills are often not easy for a child from a good economic background to achieve. They are especially difficult for the child who has limited experiences due to socioeconomic deprivation.

The majority of pre-elementary school children begin instruction with certain deficiencies:

(1) limited knowledge of mathematical concepts (Although there are enough objects in the homes to help acquire form discrimination, parents do not take time to discuss arithmetic concepts.); (2) limited knowledge concerning the use of money; (3) inability to read mathematical problems (they have not yet begun to read); (4) limited ability to relate arithmetic to everyday experiences; (5) limited use of time concepts.

The following pages present a program of pre-elementary school education which will assist young children in mastering certain arithmetic concepts.

[63]

In level number one, no number names are used and no number symbols are seen. This initial level consists of matching exercises and various games played with certain devices, the object being to use games as a means of developing a child's number sense.

The matching exercises consist of the child arranging objects in the same way the teacher has arranged them. Blocks are very good objects to use in these exercises because they are easy for the child to manipulate. An identical number of blocks should be placed before the teacher and child. The teacher then begins by pushing one block forward and indicating to the child that he is to do this also. This exercise is repeated with the teacher using a different number of blocks each time.

When the child has mastered this exercise, the teacher can introduce the second phase of level one. The child will be given a piece of construction paper which has a certain number of objects—also made of construction paper, and of various sizes—pasted to it. (The objects also should be of a color contrasting with that of the background paper.) The child will then be given the proper materials and told to make a card like the one the teacher has given him. This is to be repeated, with the number of objects on each card becoming increasingly difficult. All children will not be able to do this, and the teacher should not push a child who displays that he is not ready for this task.

The second level in this method of arithmetic instruction is concerned with the introduction of numbers. Numbers one through ten are first learned by associating the numerals with objects. The child may count chairs or other children.

This method of instruction will be more meaningful to children if work and play are combined in presenting ordinal numbers. The teacher should say, "Numbers are words we use every day. We say them like this—'One, two, three, four.' " She should then repeat the numbers. After doing this several times slowly, she counts several children; then she asks the class to do this with her. This is to be repeated over and over.

Rhythmic movements may be added to give the learning situation variety. The children can swing their arms or clap their hands while they count.

After the first four or five numbers have been introduced, and the children verbally familiar with them, the teacher can present them visually. The numbers should be written on the board. As she writes the number, she must say the number's name. The teacher should then point to each number and say its name again. After this has been done several times, she should ask the class to repeat the names with her as she points to the numbers. Individual members of the class may be called forward to do this with the teacher.

When the children have repeated this exercise several times, the teacher may say, "I am going to point to the numbers on the board and you say, 'One, two, three, four, or five.' At the same time you will quietly stand up and sit down with the rhythm of the numbers. Do it like this." The teacher demonstrates. The movements should be changed fairly often to add variety to the exercise. The teacher should limit the movements to those which are not too loud because too much noise distracts from the order of the exercise.

Children enjoy making rhymes as they drill with numbers. The teacher could say, "Number words can be fun words. Listen. One, two, look at my shoe." After the children have learned this rhyme, they can use it in many ways. They can use it individually or in groups. They should also be encouraged to make up their own rhymes. The children may add rhythmic movements and play classroom games. As an example, the teacher can begin the games by saying, "One, two, three, four—Johnny, would you please open the door?" At this time, the child whose name was called comes forward and opens the classroom door. On the door are number symbols written on a sheet of paper. He identifies the four numbers. If he is correct, he will then repeat the rhyme using another child's name in the class.

After the class appears to be familiar with the first five numbers, the next five numbers should be introduced. The same procedure may be followed in teaching these number names and symbols.

When the class has learned to verbalize and recognize all numbers, they should learn to write the number symbols.

Next, the children should work on fine motor coordination. They should practice making straight lines, circles, squares and curves while using crayons on cardboard. The teacher should observe each child as he does this work, and help those who encounter difficulty. When the children appear to have no trouble working with cardboard patterns, they should then begin to draw designs on paper.

When freehand drawing of these designs is no longer difficult for the children, they are ready to write the numerals. The teacher should say, "The name for numbers which we write is 'numeral.' Today we will learn to write the numerals one, four, and seven. Each of these numerals is made with a straight line." The teacher then writes "one," "four," and "seven" on the board. Then she writes the remaining seven numerals from one through ten on the board and asks the children to point out other numerals made with straight lines. Children need to use rulers when they first begin, in order to make their lines straight.

The teacher will next write the numeral two on the board. She asks the children in what way numeral two is different from numerals one, four, and seven.

The "eight" is the next numeral introduced to the class. The teacher will draw the "eight" on the board and say, "This is an 'eight.' We make this numeral by making one circle on top and another on the bottom, or by making an 'S' forward and then an 'S' backwards. Also, you may draw a circle using a penny; then move the penny down and draw another circle."

The teacher describes the "nine" as a small egg-shaped circle with a straight line drawn down from the right side. It would be appropriate for the children to draw eggs, discuss chickens, and a host of other things whereby the numerical nine can be tied to actual experiences.

When the children are no longer having difficulty in writing these six numbers, the four remaining ones may be introduced. The "two" may be described as a candy cane with a flat tail at the bottom. This would follow some activity where all children are rewarded for some performance by giving them a candy cane which, of course, looks like the numeral two.

The "six" is said to begin with a straight line going down and finishes with a small egg-like circle on the bottom right-hand side.

The "five" is introduced by the teacher writing a "five" on a blackboard. After writing the figure on the board, the teacher should say that the "five" has two straight lines and a half-circle.

Two pennies should be used, when the instruction begins, concerning the numeral three. The pennies are placed one above the other. With a pencil, the child can trace around the right-hand side of the coins. This, of course, makes a perfect numerical three.

The teacher then asks the children what other numeral can be made with pennies. The children are encouraged to use the pennies to make the number eight.

After these aspects of numbers one through ten have been learned thoroughly by the children, the concept of numerical order should be presented by the teacher. They will already have a slight knowledge of this concept since they learned the number names in order. If the children are to learn the significance of order, the teacher must have them do a project on a vehicle having many cars, such as a train. Such a project here is to present the idea that the train begins with an engine and ends with a caboose, and has many cars between the two.

The teacher should begin by writing, in numerical order, the numbers one through ten on the board, and then point to each number on the board, pronounce the number, and have the class repeat the numerical names. She should then say, "This is the order of the numbers. It is very much like a train. If the numbers are not written like this, they are not in the correct order." The teacher can then use a variety of techniques such as permitting students to cut out and assign each other numbers, and then arrange themselves in a number train —insuring that the numbers are in correct order. Another technique is for one student to draw the numbers from a box. Other students can then decide on the correct order. These and other techniques should be repeated over and over until the class has an understanding of the concept of order.

After this exercise, the teacher may write the numbers in large print on poster paper and cover one of the numbers with a small card. She should ask the class, "What number is missing?" The child who is the first to answer correctly gets to cover the next number.

The concept of quantity is the next level of sequential order. A group of large wooden blocks or several balls is needed when presenting this idea. The teacher should have the blocks or balls together in groups of two, three, and four. She should also have single blocks or balls for the children to use. She should then instruct the children to point and tell how many blocks or balls are in a group. The children then touch the objects as the teacher counts them. Later, the children will count them. This is done several times so the children may observe the groupings. After this has been repeated many times, the teacher should ask one child to pick up a block in one hand, and the cluster of four blocks in the other. The teacher then asks the child to tell the class how many blocks he has in each hand.

Next, the teacher could ask, "Which weighs more?" This should be done by several children and the class should determine that four blocks weigh more than one. The teacher should say that "one" is a small number, and "four" is bigger than "one." This should be stressed over and over, with different numbers of blocks or balls being used, before the teacher uses the abstract number sysmbols in connection with this concept.

The mathematical concepts which have been discussed on the preceding pages are examples of those ideas which a teacher must literally spell out for the pre-elementary school child. Instruction of these concepts must always begin in the concrete form, as they have been presented here, and then, as the children are ready, move to a more abstract form. If the concepts which have been introduced in this method of instruction are learned thoroughly by the children in a pre-elementary school class, they will be much better equipped to enter first grade.

DEVELOPMENT OF STUDY HABITS

It is essential that young children learn an effective method of study. Since arithmetic is a fundamental subject, effective study habits require that the learner become self-reliant, and that he continually pose questions to himself, such as "Why?" and "How?" Although young children should continually query themselves, they also need the guidance of the teacher. They should not be required to work long periods on their own, but rather, to work brief periods (about fifteen minutes for pre-elementary school pupils). The periods of self-work should be followed by teacher guidance and consultation.

The teacher should encourage and permit each child to try and work at his own level. The child's effort must be accepted by the teacher, and he should be encouraged, even though he has given the wrong answer. Let the child come up with *how to do it*. This is not only a challenge to the child, but also to the teacher.

PROBLEM SOLVING

Problem solving is an important part of the arithmetic program from the very beginning of the child's experiences in school. As already stated, the teacher must begin with the concrete and move slowly to the abstract. Young children tend to see things in action (physical situations). Therefore, such a situation should be used for maximum learning conditions. The child should be taught to describe the situation, and in describing it, he should be encouraged to use arithmetic symbols. In this way, the symbols represent the numbers involved, as well as the action implied.

RANGE OF ABILITIES

Some children require many concrete experiences to master arithmetical ideas. Others tire quickly of such activities and need more encouragement from the teacher, and more challenging experiences. The teacher working with pre-elementary school children, though, should be encouraged in knowing that the range of abilities will be lower at this level than at most any level in the school situation. Children should really want to participate—to learn, to find the answer— if the classroom situation is fertile and conducive to inquiry. Each child must do his own learning, and the teacher is there to guide, encourage, and aid. The freedom of approach and the possibility of success will produce the needed interest. There must be a great amount of success to feed the desire to learn, and to try again. This does not mean there will not be failure, but failure should be held to a minimum and the children rewarded for their efforts. We can say that almost all children can learn, and the majority will respond to the suggested teaching procedures.

EVALUATION

Even at the pre-elementary school level, the teacher must have some formal and informal means of evaluating the individual pupil's progress, and of recording such progress. It must be pointed out that, at this level, young children should be evaluated more on an informal basis than a formal one. The teacher should construct her own work-sheets which indicate how well the child is doing. These worksheets are administered to the class only so the teacher can help each child progress at his ability level.

Evaluation must be continuous, it cannot be separated from teaching, it must be geared to the needs of the children, and it must be used as an aid to all the children.

THE USE OF SYMBOLS

Many authorities believe that arithmetic language should be developed in the same way that all language is developed. This order is listening, speaking, familiarity with objects, action, and finally, descriptive words. It is very important for the child to build a listening and speaking arithmetic vocabulary before he attempts reading the words or symbols. It then follows that symbols should be introduced after the children have become acquainted with the idea that was first presented. It should be stressed that teaching the use of symbols can be done with meaning, and need not be done as a rote procedure. A child can even learn to count from one through ten with real meaning if he begins counting objects, rather than just repeating "One, two, three, four, etc." over and over. Teachers must remember also that vocabulary comes first, followed by the symbols; then comes the understanding of ideas, followed by the expression of principles.

STRUCTURE

When young students learn the structure of arithmetic, they learn how its phases are related, and they see that a specific topic is related to the total structure of arithmetic. The following passage points out the importance of a systematic pattern in learning arithmetic:

> It is easier to memorize words than nonsense syllables. It is easier to memorize numbers expressed with digits in a systematic pattern than in a random sequence. In like manner, learning in mathematics is accomplished most economically and effectively when the emphasis is on structure and on relationships and organization in what is learned. (Marks, Purdy, and Kinney, 1965).

DISCOVERY APPROACH

The discovery approach has received a great deal of attention in recent years, and the new mathematics programs have emphasized it a great deal. Perhaps it would be best to sum up the philosophy of teaching mathematics by a quote from Bruner (1965) concerning the discovery approach.

> For whether one speaks to mathematicians, or physicists, or historians, one encounters repeatedly an expression of faith in the powerful effects that come from permitting the student to put things together for himself, to be his own discoverer.

REFERENCES

Bruner, Jerome S.: The act of discovery. In Anderson, Richard C., and Ausubel, David P.: *Readings in the Psychology of Cognition.* New York, Hold, Rinehart and Winston, 1965, p. 607.

Marks, John L.; Purdy, C. Richard, and Kinney, Lucien B.: *Teaching Elementary School Mathematics for Understanding,* 2nd ed. New York, McGraw-Hill, 1965, p. 11.

Chapter 6

PREPARING CHILDREN FOR READING

ALL CHILDREN NEED to be prepared for the act of reading, and an adequate background is important. The general estimate of severe reading disability among school children is 15 to 20 percent, and among educationally deprived children the disability estimate is as high as 50 percent. Best estimates indicate, then, unless we do something, as many as half of our children will develop reading problems. The answer appears to lie in an enriched pre-elementary school program of one or more years for most children.

Pre-elementary school programs for children vary from area to area. However, the following points apply to all programs: (1) there is a greater length of time usually required by disadvantaged children to be ready for reading instruction; (2) a great emphasis should be placed on language experiences; (3) the children should have a wide variety of experiences, especially field trips, and (4) communications between all the children and the teacher is a must.

Since most pre-elementary school programs will be racially integrated, teachers must exercise judgment in the selection of pictures and storybooks. Black children from impoverished areas are more likely to respond to pictures and stories which relate to familiar activities and characters, than to stories and pictures which do not.

A pre-elementary school program should teach children how to get along with others, have and keep good health, develop and keep a sense of orderliness, be oneself, and be ready for the thinking exercises in school.

It should be noted that much debate surrounds the topic of pre-elementary school programs concerned with reading readiness. A pre-elementary school class should provide a variety of material for experimentation and manipulation. It should extend the chance to acquire information and understanding about people and things, but most important it should provide opportunities for children to solve problems and correct misconceptions.

"Why should I force children to grow up too fast?

"I can teach many young children to read, but it could do them more harm than good.

"They will just have to be taught the same things later when they are really ready."

These are a few of the arguments that are considered when preparing young children for reading.

Most good research conducted in the area of young children being taught reading indicates that arguments against early reading are more myth than fact. Pre-elementary children are ripe for preparation for reading. Those not given the chance to read are apt to develop reading problems.

Those opposed to teaching young children to read probably find it easy to discard recent research for no apparent reason. For example, some educators claim the various programs were developed under isolated laboratory conditions, based on a highly selective cross section of children, involved a lot of expensive gadgets and gimmicks, and are inappropriate for any number of imagined reasons.

The Denver project, for example, really cannot be overlooked, for there were no tricks. Instead, there was a dedicated project staff, sound reading program materials, teachers willing to work, and a study group so large that it was bound to include a representative sample of children. The study indicated that the average and below average benefited from early reading, not just a selected few. Other studies are presently being conducted along the lines of the Denver research.

A pre-elementary school program can help prepare children to read in the same way it readies them for all school life—by broadening the base of their knowledge.

Nothing is more essential to later success in reading than a wealth of concepts which adds meaning to the printed symbol. If we deprive young children the opportunity to gain this breadth of understanding, we actually make the reading process more difficult later.

In preparing young children for reading, it is important that a systematic plan of instruction be followed. This plan should:

(1) build a healthy self-concept through successful accomplishments; (2) teach children to communicate with all types of people;

(3) develop ability to associate the meaning of many words with activities related to life; (4) develop understanding of the meaning of words through real experiences; (5) aid children to discern likeness and differences; (6) assist children to become aware of and enjoy sounds of rhyming words; (7) stimulate conversation with others; (8) encourage recognition of words by attaching meaning to the printed symbol; (9) teach the children that written words convey meaning; (10) help children understand that reading is fun and essential for a full life.

Readiness Activities

Readiness for beginning reading skills depends on the cultivation of the potential sources of prereading experiences which exist in every preelementary classroom. The following are examples of readiness activities which are effective because they provide the raw material on which oral language and reading are based:

1. A variety of experiences are provided which increase the children's fund of language meaning. These may include orientation trips to city office buildings, trips in the immediate neighborhood to locate various things found in the community, or trips to the farm, zoo, and similar places in the community which appeal to young children.

2. Music activities, songs, and games provide opportunities for using and interpreting language.

3. Poems and literature are useful in developing interest in books and reading. Children are encouraged to choose books for the teacher to read, and then to discuss their favorite stories. While reading the stories to the children, the teacher is developing the idea that the printed word tells a story. She may occasionally write a word on the board, pronounce it, and have the children raise their hands when she reads the word in the story.

4. Dramatization and other oral language activities are very important in helping to increase language development.

Interesting Activities

Examples of experiences and activities related to interests of children are as follows:

1. A large booklet may be made with the title, "Our Friends and Pets." In preparing such a booklet, the teacher should record stories

which the children make up about their pets. By using their words and phrases, the teacher helps the children sense the linkage between the spoken and written word. The children should also draw pictures or bring in photographs and magazine cutouts for a book about pets. Upon completion, such a book can be kept and enjoyed as part of the room library. Later it will be taken home for the family to see.

2. A trip to a nearby supermarket could set off a discussion on foods and food values. Children could then browse through magazines, choosing representative foods—vegetables, meats, and desserts—and arrange them in labeled order. These may be assembled on a large chart, in a group booklet, or in individual booklets.

3. Many children enjoy talking about their families. After an "interview" at home with his father and mother, the child may contribute an illustrated page for a classroom booklet on "How My Parents Help." Written explanatory captions may accompany each picture. Individual pictures may be painted or drawn of family groups with a caption, such as "This is My Family" or "This Is My Brother or Sister."

Visual Activities

The following books, games, and puzzles are helpful in developing specific visual skills necessary for success in reading:

1. Books: *Mother Goose, The Three Bears, Jack and Jill, Little Red Riding Hood,* etc. Have the class members dramatize the characters in a popular book or rhyme and present the class play at "family night."

2. Sequence puzzles, both commercial and teacher-made: Children must know the stories well and understand the plot in order to put the events in sequential order. Frequently, they are based on fairy tales. Observing children work the various games gives the teacher clues to children's stages of readiness for beginning reading.

3. Matching games: "Match-up" is a familiar example of the kind of games in which pictures are paired. The children begin with simple picture-matching games and later progress to matching words and pictures. Eventually, they are able to match words or phrases, and even short sentences, without the picture clues.

4. "Lotto" and "Wordo": There are many picture lotto games and word games available commercially, or the teacher may devise

her own sets. As reading skills develop, children are ready for lotto games using words and phrases.

5. Story games: Some teachers devise games which are played in the manner of many of the commercial games. The game board may be an original one—say, about "The Three Bears." These games are helpful in developing reading readiness and color discrimination, as well as readiness in other academic areas.

6. Other picture-clue games: Many games may be devised for nurturing picture interpretation skills. Games may be made which are helpful in developing the child's ability to organize. Game boards with pockets can be constructed by the children and the teacher. A picture clue is inserted at the left of each pocket and a stack of cards placed in the pockets according to the category picture clue. Endless varieties of this game may be devised concerning such subjects as foods, pets, zoo animals, transportation, and so forth.

7. The picture file: Picture files are used by most kindergarten-primary teachers. The teacher may place three, four or five cards in a pocket chart and say, "These are pictures of animals you know. Which ones did you see at the zoo?" Or she may ask, "Can you find two animals whose names rhyme?"

8. Jingles: The teacher recites part of a jingle, does an imitation of the unfinished portion, and the children guess the answer.

SAMPLE TEACHER-MADE WORKSHEETS

1. "Saw" and "was": The object is to increase perception of children to the correct form through thinking, hearing, and vision. The children are seated in a circle with the teacher, who holds ten cards, each bearing the words "saw" and "was." One by one, the cards are passed out to the class. Tommy is asked to stand and display his card. All children having a similar card are asked to stand. The teacher can provide variations of the game.

2. "Did" and "do": The cards are first displayed to the children. The teacher, with children in a circle, asks each one to think of something he or she did the previous day.

Teacher: "What did you do, Jimmy?"

Jimmy: "I went to the store."

Teacher: "When did you do it?"

Jimmy: "I did it yesterday."
There are hundreds of variations of similar games.

Teaching Principles

There are many teaching principles which apply to all children, but there are a few which are particularly applicable to young children:

1. Utilize all of the child's senses: visual, olfactory, tactile, and gustatory. The pre-elementary school should insure that each child has had an eye test and an audiometer check.

2. Begin with things known to the child because known things form a solid base to include the less familiar. The intangibles can then be brought into the picture.

3. Activities should start with simple concepts and skills, because the child possibly could be overwhelmed if he is permitted to touch and explore too wide a variety of objects and things in too short a time.

Development of the following areas will assist young children in becoming successful readers when they enter school: (1) language, (2) experiences, (3) perception—visual and auditory, and (4) new and old concepts.

LANGUAGE

Some children enter school with a smaller vocabulary than the average child, but also, the language he uses can be in conflict with the language used in the school. It is the job of the teacher to become familiar with the language differences of the children. If the teacher approaches the child's level by learning the child's means of expression, she can build a bridge of communication between herself, the child, and the other children. These children should not be asked to give up their language, but instead, to gradually enrich their language and add to it.

Perhaps the best way for the child to become familiar with correct and usable language is to hear it over and over again through the use of stories. Choose one section of the classroom as a storytelling corner and cover it with a pallet for the children to sit on. The teacher should sit on a low-enough chair so all the children can easily see and hear her. Storytelling periods should be varied between reading stories from books, telling stories, and using the flannelboard to depict stories visually. This not only encourages good English usage, but also promotes a base for building reading readiness skills.

Since books play such an important part in increasing the child's awareness of, and interest in, language, he should be taught respect for these books and how to handle them. Getting to look at a book on his own should be a privilege for a child, not something to do when everything else has been done. Books should be used as a reward that becomes the child's own possession to take home and share with the family—if he chooses.

Field trips, filmstrips, or slides provide an excellent means of broadening the child's background. Filmstrips which are both entertaining and informative are available from numerous companies on any subject the teacher can imagine. Slides are also available, although teacher-made slides of the child's environment may be even more valuable than those that are commercially prepared.

PERCEPTION

Visual memory and discrimination. Before a child is able to read, he must first learn to note differences and similarities between objects before he is able to distinguish one word from another. This is known as visual discrimination. When the child begins to build a sight vocabulary, he must be able to remember those words he has seen before. Therefore, his visual memory comes into play. The following are various types of activities designed to stimulate and improve visual memory and discrimination:

1. Play a game in which all children sit in a circle and close their eyes. One child leaves the room, and the other children must open their eyes and guess who has left (visual memory). The child comes back in and chooses the next child to leave the room by touching him on the shoulder with a pointer. (All the other children have their eyes shut.)

2. A variation of the first activity would be to place four objects in front of the children, and then cover them up to see how many the children can remember.

3. Take the children for a walk, telling them beforehand to be

especially observant of everything they see. Later, discuss several of the things they saw.

4. Have the children look at pictures which are then covered to see how many details they can remember.

Auditory memory and discrimination. Also necessary for reading readiness is the development of auditory memory and discrimination. These skills help the child learn to pronounce words through the sounds they make. Many young childen have been surrounded by so much noise in their environment that they have learned to tune sounds out. Therefore, they may lack listening skills when they come to the pre-elementary school. If the teacher plans to develop good listening habits among the children, she must first listen to them. All people like to be heard, and the good teacher is not only a good instructor, but also a good listening board.

The teacher and youngsters should take a tape recorder into the neighborhood and tape familiar sounds for the children to identify. The children should close their eyes and listen to sounds in the classroom. Repeat this activity outside and compare the different sounds (auditory discrimination).

To practice perceiving and locating sounds, have a child stand approximately in the center of the classroom with another child in each corner. One of the corner children claps his hands or makes a sound, and the child in the center must guess who made the noise (auditory discrimination).

The teacher should have the youngsters play games whereby the children must identify words that sound alike at the beginning, such as farm, fire, frog, far, front, etc.

CONCEPTS

Being able to make associations, and to think logically and clearly, are facets of the child's reading readiness development which must not be neglected if he is to learn to read. The following are some aids to concept development:

1. The children must learn to follow directions. Begin with a simple direction and increase to several directions that the child must learn to carry out in order, such as, "Close the window, put the book on the desk, bring me that pencil, shut the door, and pick up the paper."

2. Keep packets of pictures available for children to classify. One packet might contain pictures of animals and another, pictures of clothes cut from a catalog.

3. Have the children choose objects which are rough and smooth, and hard and soft. The children will all be blindfolded, except one child who will hold the object and have one of the blindfolded children rub it. The child, of course, says aloud whether or not it is rough or smooth, or hard or soft.

Teaching pre-elementary school children can be very rewarding and a lot of fun, but it is also hard work. Teachers can prepare themselves for working with young children, or any other type of child for that matter, by spending a few spare hours in making materials which will serve as invaluable aids to their teaching.

Of prime importance is a picture file. Separate sections will be needed for pictures used in sequencing, puzzles, classification, and storytelling. In some cases, a set of large pictures may be needed for group work, and a set of small pictures for individual work.

READING AND CHILD DEVELOPMENT

Just as individuals learning to drive a car are at first concerned and preoccupied with the mechanics of shifting the gear and turning the wheel just enough to make the corner, a child at first is concerned with the mechanics of reading—starting at the left and going across the line, starting at the top and going downward, differentiating "cat" from "dog," remembering the sounds of letters are some of the mechanics of reading.

Later, just as individuals learn to drive without a conscious effort, a child will develop reading skills which become seemingly automatic until he reaches a point where he can read almost any word he sees without having seen or heard the word before.

Reading is more than just saying sounds that match symbols. Symbols are nothing until they mean something to somebody. So the words a child reads must have meaning for him. Written words come alive as a child sees them under a colorful picture of a familiar object, or as he sees his name either over the locker where his coat hangs or posted on his possessions. He lives his words as he counts out paper for each child, or distributes the drinking straws at milk time.

He is reading when, at age four or five, he selects his favorite record from a stack of eight when they all have the same red labels. The child is reading because he is discriminating likes and differences, and using certain clues to recognize the object for which he searched. When a child reads from the printed page, he is using similar clues— except that they are more abstract and subtle.

Reading, then, is the process of securing meaning from printed words. It is a key that unlocks doors. Doors of self-esteem, peer acceptance, new information, recreation, future happiness, and success are opened in proportion to the reading skills which the child possesses.

Being ready to read doesn't happen as soon as the child enters school. He has been working toward this goal in language development since his birth.

Reading, like child growth, is developmental. Growth is a process of enlargement, without a noticeable change in complexity. When something grows, it stays the same—except for getting larger. Development, on the other hand, indicates a sequential unfolding and gradual change in complexity. If begun at the right time and with the essentials, reading and child development occur simultaneously and painlessly. As the child develops physically, mentally, socially, and emotionally, reading takes its place at the proper time.

Chapter 7

PARAEDUCATIONAL PERSONNEL

THE LABELING PROCESS

O NE OF THE TRENDS of the last several years has been an increasing dissatisfaction with diagnostic procedures. The tendency to brand and label is extremely prevalent in our society. Children are labeled and grouped homogeneously in the nation's schools on the basis of these diagnostic stamps which are provided by a number of people, some well-trained, some not well-trained.

Teachers have come to cherish these labels, guard them, and even pass them on to other teachers. These teachers, in turn, quickly pass them on to other people. Because of the emphasis placed on testing in our colleges and universities, teachers sometime see imaginary differences between the children in their classes.

It is true that educators and psychologists have heralded the team approach for many years, but only in rare cases have the diagnostic reports been followed by remedial procedures. Often the entire team does not see the child, but only one or two members on the team do the diagnosis. The result has been, though, to label him mentally retarded, emotionally disturbed, brain-injured or some other such derogatory thing.

Many people who have worked in such a multidisciplinary approach contend it is an ideal seldom attained in practice. Investigation points out that such diagnostic clinics came into being as a result of pressure applied by parents, and not because of a direct need from school programs. Critics assert that few pre-elementary school, culturally deprived children can be diagnosed correctly because the instruments used are biased against them. They are culturally loaded instruments. For the most part, these children are neurophysiologically normal and generally test in the low average range prior to school entrance. At the time they start to school, however, they test as mildly retarded on instruments such as the Stanford-Binet or Wechsler Intelligence Scale for Children (WISC) because there measures are "educationally loaded." It is in the area of complex abilities that these children are most deficient because of their poor backgrounds.

Actually, the followers of this point of view maintain that the school situation makes these children mentally retarded because of the cultural deficiency that it imposes on them. Diagnosis often stops when psychological reasons and causation are identified, the child is placed in a special class, and this has been justified in the eyes of the team members. The child usually stays in the special class.

The recent trend to test children earlier, say at age three or four, will tend to label the child earlier than in the past, and probably will contribute more than any one thing to a lag in development.

Usually, the diagnosis of mental retardation is considered to have been made when a school counselor or psychologist has administered an intelligence test to a child, and has obtained an intelligence quotient score below some cut-off point (usually IQ 75), the main purpose being to brand the child and justify his placement in a special class. Dunn (1968) states: "In large measure, this has resulted in digging the educational graves of many racially and/or economically disadvantaged children by using a WISC or Binet intelligence quotient score to justify the label 'mentally retarded.' "

Wolf Wolfensberger (1965) is very critical of the present diagnostic procedures being used to identify children, and particularly, mental retardation. He calls attention to five practices that he labels as "embarrassments" to the field of special education. Four of these are as follows:

(1) Diagnosis is quite often a dead-end for the family. Instead of leading to a meaningful service assignment, it frequently results only in a frustrating series of fruitless cross-referrals.

(2) Many diagnostic centers do not provide adequate feedback counseling, considering their duty done the moment the diagnostic process is completed to their satisfaction.

(3) Diagnostic services are often overdeveloped in comparison to other available resources.

(4) According to theory and cliche, it is of utmost importance that diagnosis take place as early as possible. In practice, however, early diagnosis can be a disaster. A child diagnosed as retarded at or near birth may never find the crucial initial acceptance, and may be viewed with conflict attitudes which prevent the formation of deep parental love.

Wolfensberger calls for a family-centered attitude on the part of the diagnostic team. Traditionally, the approach has been staff-centered. He also believes we should take a close look at the practices in the much-praised, but often inadequate, team approach.

One of the chief criticisms of the team approach is that too often the problem becomes one not of education, but of a multitude of things. Also, too often, remediation is not available and often is not possible, according to the diagnosis. Many of the psychologists who recommend remediation have not taught in public or private schools.

Seymor Sarason (1960) calls attention to the need for community diagnostic facilities, and to the failure of professionals to provide parents and educators with a realistic understanding of the child's capacities. This writer particularly likes Sarason's suggestion number two, wherein he said the following criteria might be considered essential to the evaluation of mental subnormality—ideal in the sense that an awareness of these essentials may tend at least to set limits on reckless diagnosis: (1) an intellectual and social assessment of the present functioning of the child; (2) data relating to the development of major problems in the life of the child (these may be psychological, physical, medical, etc.); (3) an evaluation of the neurologic status of the child.

The writer would like to add a fourth and fifth essential to the above list: (4) an educational evaluation by an educator, and (5) a prediction of the potential of the child if he is given the proper school situation and a moderate change in environment.

EVIDENCE AGAINST USING AN INDIVIDUAL INTELLIGENCE SCORE FOR PLACEMENT

It is said that individual intelligence tests measure performance, and also allow the opportunity for the examiner to observe behavior in a standard testing situation. Naturally, education is important in a child's score. The performance score provides a basis for comparison of the child's perfomance with that of other members of his age group, but not his socioeconomic level. The possible level of comparison should be a value to teachers, but too often the comparison is unfair because of individual differences in environment. As of this date, though, there are no perfect measures of ability, and there is good reason to believe that we will never have such.

A child's ability in a particular activity cannot be adequately measured every day, because no arbitrary standards can be set which will have the same validity at all times. Therefore, what is being measured is his performance on a particular day. The performance of a particular child at this time does not guarantee that a future performance will be the same, or that success will be the same on that, or any other type of test.

The intelligence quotient, used as a ratio to indicate performance which is relative to a child's age, is valuable, but should be used with discretion. No child has an intelligence quotient that is static—rather, he has ratio scores on every test he takes. These scores may differ greatly, and often we pick a low score and "brand" the child with it. From the point of view of Louttit (1957), the "observed behavior is perhaps a more important value of tests than the numerical scores alone." Sarason (1960) places emphasis on the fact that no one functions at a measured intelligence quotient at all times, and in all situations.

Information possessed by human beings about a child's IQ often affects him adversely. What is expected of a child tends to determine his success or failure. This is known as the "self-fulfilling prophesy," the occurrence having been demonstrated by Rosenthal and Jacobson (1968). These two conducted research that is relevant to intelligence testing.

Eighteen elementary teachers were used, covering three classes of each grade level from one to six. The teachers were given the names of children identified as academic "spurters," and were told that the children had hidden talent. The teachers then expected these children would progress more rapidly during the school year than other children in the class. The names had been selected at random, and no tests had actually been given. All the children were tested after the teachers were told about the "spurters." When the children were retested eight months later, the results showed significantly larger rises in total intelligence quotients among the "spurters" than among their classmates.

The above experiment, wherein advanced IQ information was given, aroused in the teachers an expectation of differences in academic progress. The experiment also revealed that branding a child with a low intelligence score has a similar effect in that it reduces the teacher's expectancy for him.

A very profound criticism of intelligence tests is that they brand a child permanently. A low IQ stamps "inferiority" on a child. In the case of socially disadvantaged children, a low intelligence quotient score often accentuates their handicaps.

Because of the above reasons, and probably many more, group intelligence tests in the New York City public schools were discontinued in 1964.

It cannot be stressed enough that the use of an intelligence test score must not be treated casually, for in addition to possibly branding a person for life, it often affects the course of a child's life by determining the education and training the child will receive, and how people will act toward the individual involved. California is omitting the title "special class" because of the implication.

Most psychologists agree that the idea of a culture-free or pure measure of intelligence has been abandoned as impossible. It is an accepted fact that abilities can be estimated only after they develop. This development is not a simple matter of the unfolding of native capacities, but is determined by the result of learning processes in which the stimulation of the environment plays an important part.

Intelligence testing of children should be discouraged, except when a specific indication exists (Bakwin and Bakwin, 1963). There is very little reason to test a normal child—and there are disadvantages. Besides, numerical rating of intelligence has only relative accuracy. By permitting seemingly precise comparisons, it encourages an attitude of competition among mothers and could lead to needless parental concern, disappointment and anxiety.

There are, however, situations in which intelligence testing is useful. An intelligence score is useful in detecting retarded children in doubtful cases. In addition, it is an indication of the extent of the retardation, and could indicate how it affects the child's adjustment in other respects. It must be emphasized, though, that this test is not to be used to label the child throughout his school career.

Intelligence testing can be very useful in counseling with academically retarded children who are suspected to have average-or-above intelligence.

McGaugh (1968) reports that it is time to discard intelligence tests as we presently know them, and time to develop tests designed to assess specific processes of learning and memory. Such tests could be used to diagnose individual differences in learning efficiency, and could prove useful in helping develop teaching practices designed to deal with individual differences in learning and memory.

A mental-ability test which measures readiness for academic subjects could be of value as a replacement for the intelligence test. This test would not have a numerical score, but would indicate when the child is ready to compete in the first grade. In this way, the term "readiness" would not apply to a static situation.

A CLINICAL APPROACH TO REPLACING CURRENT DIAGNOSTIC PROCEDURES

In the area of handicapped children, Dunn (1968) contends that the present diagnostic procedures should be replaced by expecting special educators to be responsible for their own diagnostic and clinical teaching. This, of course, also can be applied to education in the regular classroom or more appropriately, education of the child who must always live in our society. With this in mind, he suggests that we do away with categorizing these children and grouping them homogeneously by classification into special classes.

To accomplish the above procedure, a revolution in special education will be required, according to Dunn. This is true of all education. The self-contained special classes which before have housed primarily ethnically or economically disadvantaged children labeled mentally retarded should be discontinued. According to Dunn, these children should be returned to the regular elementary grades until educators are equipped to handle their educational problems to the best advantage of the child.

The primary purpose of diagnosis in the schools is to carry out the remediation which may be psychological, medical, educational, or any combination of these. This remediation has education and adequate functioning in our society as the ultimate goal. "Prescriptive teaching is a method utilizing diagnostic information for the modification of educational programs for children with problems" (Peters, 1965). It is concerned more with the *what* of the child than with the *why* and *how*. The teacher needs to know *what* the child can learn, under *what* conditions, and with *what* materials. To accomplish this, Dunn suggests, as the most desirable administrative procedure, the establishment of a "Special Education Diagnostic and Prescription Generating Center," one for each large school system, or for two or more small school districts. According to Dunn:

> Pupils with school learning problems would be enrolled in this center on a day and/or boarding school basis for a period of time—probably up to a month, and hopefully until a successful prescription for effective teaching had been evolved. The core of the staff would be a variety of master teachers with different specialties, such as motor development, perceptual development, language development, social and personality development, remedial education, and so forth. Noneducators such as physicians, psychologists, and social workers would be retained in a consultative role, or pupils would be referred to such paraeducational professionals as needed.

FAILURE OF THE TEAM APPROACH IN THE PAST, AND POSSIBLE CORRECTIVE MEASURES

The term "paraeducational personnel" places emphasis on the role of the educator, both as an active participant in the multidisciplinary term, and as a coordinator of the learning situation. In the past, the practice has been to refer the child to various professional personnel, and as a result, teachers had a medical opinion about a child (along with bulky folders full of medical and/or psychological information) —without true knowledge of how the child functioned in the classroom. It was not unusual to see a problem, defined by a teacher as a learning problem, redefined as a health problem or personality deviation, and the road away from education in the classroom was clearly defined.

The proponents of the team approach seem to forget that a mass of clinical data about the child does not necessarily mean he will receive better instruction. Too often, teachers are presented a mass of esoteric words in the diagnostic write-up, but no solution to the child's problem. The educational problem of the child is often secondary and the teachers are ignored.

Proponents of the team approach should ask themselves whether the information gathered by physicians, psychologists, social workers, and other team members has any real bearing on the teaching process. Current practices suggest that information often says nothing to teachers—that there is a breakdown in the communication of information from one discipline to another. It would be naive to think that communication problems consist of one person's not knowing all the big words the other person uses. The problem is more complicated than that.

The difficulty concerns agreement about what matters should be raised. These questions should be asked: "What needs to be known about a child by any professional person? What can we do to help this child function better? What does the teacher need to know in order to help the child? Does categorizing help the child?"

The first step that should be taken in correcting this agreement lag is to give attention to who interprets individual and group psycho-educational tests—and we should make sure that the child benefits from any testing situation. Too often, in the past, test after test has been administered, and not one step has been taken to help the child. The tests used should yield a profile of abilities and disabilities which provide a basic level at which the child is functioning.

The references to paraeducational personnel establishes what is educationally relevant for the betterment of the child. The process then converts this into a program for teaching which is communicated first to the teacher, and then to others who are working with the child. In this way a practical effort can be made to fulfill the child's educational needs. This places the teacher in a position whereby every facet of the procedure for helping the child will be scrutinized, and whereby the teacher will always be a participant in the process.

Peters (1965) states that a more effective link is established between the area of diagnosis and the area of action within the school for the following reasons:

1. The school is the one institution where nearly all children have social contact which can be positively used—if therapeutic concepts are converted into learning terms.

2. Overcoming handicaps and most changes in behavior involve learning. Improvements in emotional state involve learning new emotional

responses, and the school has responsibility for the promotion of appropriate learning.

3. The educator's area of competency is in teaching and learning. If the relevant aspects of medical, psychiatric, psychological, and social work diagnostic findings are converted into pedagogical terms, the teacher can bring his skills to bear on the problem.

4. Coordination and integration of services in the interest of the handicapped child are most effective when areas of responsibility are defined. Differentiation of areas of competency and responsibility must be accomplished before effective integration of services can take place. Educators, then, make their contribution toward the reliefs of suffering of the maladjusted child through teaching, while other professions make contributions through their special competencies.

Research has provided advancement in psychological measurement, social work, psychiatry, and educational psychology, and these advancements are assisting in providing the educator with various types of information which help him assist the child in learning. The para-educational approach is here for some teachers. For others, it will come in the future. It exists for the teacher, both as a participant and a mediator, for the benefit of the child.

CLARIFICATION OF THE ROLE OF TEACHER

The mounting influence of psychological and sociological thinking upon education has helped introduce professional personnel from many fields into participation in the public school system. Recent progress in education has intensified the need for professional teamwork, and created interdisciplinary problems not present twenty years ago. For example, children with physical handicaps can be diagnosed as such by the time they are one or two years old. A team of physicians should advise and prescribe medical treatment to help the condition. This prescription, and the services of the medical team, may expand and reach directly into the classroom—and it should, but with the idea of helping the child in his educational setting. The physicians do not prescribe educationally, but the teacher should be given their findings so he may use them to help the child in the classroom.

In many cases, educational values and the unique role of the educator have not always been protected in this team approach. Traditionally, the educator's role has not been a picture of equality.

In working with members of other disciplines, particularly those which are considered prestige professions, the teacher often is intimidated into withdrawal. The esteemed position of the physician, the honor of the doctorate, the specific knowledge of the psychologist, and the medical background of both the social worker and therapist often makes the teacher appear to be the less-skilled member, and often feel like the less-professional member, of the team. In other words, the teacher is relegated to a second-class citizenship in the professional field, and accepts this situation. This problem of the status of teachers is deeply rooted in our society, but hopefully, it will change because of the changing role of the educator in the future.

The evolving concepts of using paraeducational personnel (such as the social worker, physician, guidance counselor, psychologist, and therapist) to expedite teaching should place emphasis on how to use the findings to aid the program for different children, but also how to work with the resource persons in deriving a sound program of action. The paraeducational team should not only be a diagnostic tool, but also a learning situation for all the participating members. When the teacher has respect for his own profession, believes that teaching is of great importance, and remains firm against attempts to play down his role, then he can educate the other team members to the importance of his role.

Although Dunn (1968) pointed out that the special teacher is surrounded by paraeducational personnel, this writer would like to emphasize the importance of paraeducational people in all facets of education.

THE ROLE AND RESPONSIBILITIES OF THE TEACHER IN THE FUTURE

The teacher will be called, "learning clinician" and will, as stated previously, be the leader of the team. Because schools will become clinics whose purposes are to provide individualized treatment for students, the teacher will not be just a teacher as we have known the role in the past, but will be a learning analyst.

In the school of the future, master learning clinicians will be responsible for coordinating the services needed for approximately one hundred to three hundred children. In various instructional units, we will find not only the paraeducational people, but teaching interns and other learning clinicians with allied backgrounds.

In the pre-elementary school, we will find not only the culture analysts and media specialists previously mentioned, but biochemical specialists whose services include biochemical therapy and memory improvement. We will also have pre-elementary school specialists working in the minischool programs, and in the pre-elementary continuum.

Because most of America's large cities, and some suburban and rural sections, contain what educators call disaster areas, educators in the future must bombard these ghetto and impoverished schools with progressive education. In the ghettos, it is feasible to start the preprimary continuum at the age of two. As stated earlier, this writer believes that in most cases, the age of two is entirely too young to start the education of the child by the educator and the paraeducational team, but in the case of the ghettos, this would be the appropriate age to start the educational process of the child. In the rural sections, the educational continuum will begin at age three or four.

When we start the pre-elementary continuum at the age of two, educators are not to label the child. If psychological tests are given, only one person should know the score, and no child should be clobbered by that score. During this educational process, the "right answer syndrome" should be discarded completely.

This chapter has sought to put the educator in the right place in our system of learning. Because true behavior modification is probably a myth, reeducation methods must start at birth. There is a possibility that this cannot be done.

REFERENCES

Bakwin, Harry, and Bakwin, Ruth: *Behavior Disorders in Children.* Philadelphia, Saunders, 1963, p. 29.

Dunn, Lloyd M.: Special education for the mildly retarded—is much of it justifiable? *Exceptional Children, 35*:5-21, 1968.

Jacobson, Lenore and Rosenthal, Robert: *Pygmalion in the Classroom.* New York, Holt, Rinehart, and Winston, 1968.

Louttit, C. M.: *Clinical Psychology of Exceptional Children.* New York, Harper and Brothers, 1957, p. 49.

Peters, Laurence J.: *Prescriptive Teaching.* New York, McGraw-Hill, 1965, pp. 1, 3, 4.

Sarason, Kenneth; Davidson, S.; Lighthall, Frederick, F.; Waite, Richard R., and Ruebush, Britton, K.: *Anxiety in Elementary School Children.* New York, John Wiley and Sons, 1960, pp. 105-110.

Wolfensberger, Wolf: Embarrassments in the diagnostic process. *Mental Retardation,* 1965, pp. 29-31.

Chapter 8

HEALTH AND SAFETY

It has been mentioned in previous chapters that the early years of life are the most important with respect to mental, emotional, and physical development. During the first five years, the child has an unbounded curiosity and a great desire to learn. His mind is receptive and absorbent, and at this stage he is probably more aware of, and responsive to, life around him than he will ever be again.

Pre-elementary school children from disadvantaged backgrounds are particularly more likely to repress their desire to learn than those from advantaged homes because of the immediate contrasts which are apparent to disadvantaged children. Deprived children will see other children easily manipulate objects which are unknown to them. Unless the teacher makes an effort to provide these children from deprived backgrounds the opportunity to catch up, they will fall further behind.

Health and safety instruction is an excellent tool which aids children to master objects, and at the same time protects them from harm and teaches them what to do in case of accidents and emergencies.

Naturally, a child's daily activities and his general development are closely related. The child's level of maturity will determine his interests and his activities, which in turn, stimulate his growth. Children learn through their play activity—and their play indicates what they have learned.

A teacher is likely to try looking beneath the surface in order to describe the child as being secure or insecure, aggressive or shy, noisy or quiet. Actually, the child's physical body is equally important, since its structure and functions denote the framework in which other kinds of development are housed. No one can expect children to be able to learn if they face such adverse conditions as hunger, lack of sleep, fatigue, disease, or impaired bodily functions.

It is sometimes said that the beginning of achievements lies in the health and safety of the pre-elementary school child. Any program which fails to recognize this principle is prone to be ineffective. All children in the pre-elementary school program should have a good medical examination, including examination of the eyes, nose, throat, lymph nodes, thyroid, and speech. This does not mean a two-minute examination, but rather, a thorough one. Up-to-date health records, showing change as change takes place, should be kept for all children.

Play is one of the most important needs of the pre-elementary school child. It is extremely valuable as an outlet for emotions and in learning about the world. Therefore, the teacher needs to master her tech-techniques for providing experiences through play so the child can freely express feelings and release energy.

Many different methods may be used to direct play development. As cited in one study (Piaget, 1954), play development was divided into several categories: (1) play may be introduced by an adult, whereby the child reacts and responds to that individual; (2) play may be self-initiated, in which case the child would participate alone; (3) play may be parallel, where a number of children share the same area but play independently; (4) play may be cooperative, where members of a group work together to achieve a common goal. The children may play games of low organization, such as tag, or games of high organization, such as team sports.

According to Piaget's study, each level of play represents a higher degree of social development. When the child reaches the level of parallel play, he must respect the other children. Even when playing in a sandbox he may do as he pleases with his own toys, but must respect the rights and privileges of other children. Even in games of low organization, the child must be prepared to follow certain rules. Then, when the child participates in games of high organization, he has to work with others for a common goal, for the good of the entire group, and not just for himself.

One of the best ways to involve all children in an activity is to make a game of it. This is true of all children as stated above, but it is especially true of the disadvantaged. These children have not experienced many things, but they have played games. Verbal communication is usually called for in games. Many games are people-centered and often are concerned with direct action and visible results. Games are usually sharply defined and structured, with clear-cut goals. The deprived child enjoys the challenge of the game and feels he can do it. This is in sharp contrast to many of the verbal tasks he is called upon to perform in the classroom. His background is important here because he has not had many of the verbal experiences, but has played games and engaged in vigorous competition.

At an early age the child begins to perceive the many aspects of the world about him. Naturally, this perceptual development takes place through the senses, including vision, hearing, touch, taste, and smell. It has long been known that perceptual development is stimulated by the environment. The differences found in socioeconomic strata probably make for differences in school learning during the first few years.

In the teaching of physical fitness, the teacher must be concerned with training the child to protect his life and health by taking proper care of himself. The practice of cleanliness, good eating habits, wearing proper clothing and getting sufficient rest are some of the immediate needs of all pre-elementary school children. Physical education may serve as an experience in which the child can carry out some of the aspects of good health behavior, as well as provide recreation and fun. Physicians say that physical activity stimulates the circulation of blood, teaches new muscular skills, and provides an opportunity for body, mind, and emotions to work together—thereby improving mental health as well as body functions.

The pre-elementary school must also be concerned with the development of fine and gross motor skills. This development involves more than maturation—it includes directing what is developing into specific channels. For example, walking, running, and hopping on one foot, then the other, aid in muscular development and control. Doing all of these to music will also develop rhythm and grace. Most of the activities promoting motor skills will affect the leg muscles. Knowing this, the teacher should introduce various leg-building exercises and games involving the use of the legs at various stages of leg muscle development.

DAILY PERSONAL HEALTH CARE

The teacher in the pre-elementary education school should be particularly cognizant of the importance of the promotion of the health of the skin, mouth, hearing, and vision among children. The principal emphasis concerning the promotion of these parts of the body is upon effective and enjoyable living. Many of the practices in the care of the body are primarily of esthetic value, as opposed to health values. Nevertheless, the esthetic aspects of these practices are extremely important for children and later for adults. They contribute indirectly to effective living.

To many children, the promotion of general body well-being is a simple matter. These people are fortunate, but they can still benefit by the activities in a pre-elementary school concerning the principles of health science in promoting a better way to enjoy life, and to care for various parts of the body. Other children will encounter special problems in body care which require a great deal of attention and special treatment.

THE SKIN

The skin is the largest organ of the body and functions in close collaboration with other body organs. It is the contact between the body and the outside environment, and it is extremely important to the human being. The teacher can actually teach the child about the skin and skin care in daily living. The skin is a cooling system in the summer and a heating system for the body in the winter. The function of the body depends upon a healthy skin which promotes proper circulation. The blood must carry the heat to the body surface in order to eliminate it in the summer. Children should know that the evaporation of water from the skin pulls heat from the body. they should also know that the body must have well-functioning sweat glands which will help eliminate the heat. In the winter, the children can be told that in order to conserve heat the vessels of the skin contract, thus reducing the amount of body heat that comes to the surface.

The skin must be clean and properly cared for, and the children in the pre-elementary school classes should keep charts on daily bathing and care for the skin. They should know that the skin should be soft and moderately oily, free from eruptions, and that it should not crack and scale. As the years go by, the children can be told the skin is no longer as elastic as it once was, but not to worry because it happens to all people.

ORAL HYGIENE

A healthy mouth is one which is free from defects and infections, and whose tissues function properly and efficiently. Such an oral cavity is of esthetic and social, as well as healthy, value. The oral cavity is subjected daily to many hazards and should be in good condition to withstand all of the hazards and traumas associated with daily living.

Good dental health is a combination of inheritance and proper care. Some individuals inherit good teeth and through proper care keep their teeth all of their life. Other individuals do not inherit such good teeth, but through proper care keep them for a long time. Some individuals inherit good teeth, and through poor care, lose them too soon. Other individuals inherit poor teeth and, even with good care, lose some of them.

NUTRITION

Nutrition is very important to formation of teeth, and if certain vitamins and calcium and phosphorus are omitted during the first few years when the teeth are forming, then the individual will have poor teeth. After the childhood years, though, nutrition has very little effects on tooth structure. Poor nutrition does have an effect upon gums, and vitamin C is extremely important at all ages for gum function. The child should know that carbohydrates in the mouth provide a medium for bacteria, and if these carbohydrates in the mouth remain there before and after brushing, then, of course, they will have a relationship with dental caries.

DENTAL EXAMINATIONS

The child should know that he should visit the dentist at least twice a year. During this time he should not only have an examination, but also should have his teeth cleaned. If the dentist finds that there are other things wrong with his teeth, then, of course, these will be repaired.

TOOTH BRUSHING

This should be discussed a great deal in the pre-elementary school because the school can do a lot to get each child to brush his teeth properly. The teacher should demonstrate the proper way to brush the teeth and have the children even bring tooth brushes to school in order to practice brushing correctly. The teacher should also have the children make a chart to put on the wall at home so they can mark the number of times each day they brush their teeth.

The children should be told that the toothbrush should be moderately stiff and have a small head and a straight handle. Naturally, brushing should be from the gums to the tips of the teeth.

PREVENTION OF DISEASE

Since the beginning of recorded history, mankind's struggle against disease has played an important role in the course of nations. Disease is universal and affects the whole realm of living things—both plant and animal. Therefore, in many cases, man is united in his effort to combat a particular disease which might threaten cities, nations, or even the entire world.

Because of a lack of scientific knowledge, man's early battles against disease were limited, and many times treatment of the patient was turned over to religious sects professing to have magic powers. Sanitation and prevention have, however, been practiced in limited ways since early history.

Some of the early civilizations and races developed wells, irrigation systems, baths, and sewer systems. For example, the Romans devised water carriage sewers, aqueducts, and elaborate baths. Also, the Hebrews practiced a system of personal hygiene which became a part of their religion.

During the Dark Ages, however, these practices and systems were lost. Disease flourished and the death rate was enormously high. Research reveals that the street level in some of the walled cities grew some five of six feet during this period because of the accumulation of dirt and filth. Disease gained a strong grip on man, and even after the conditions were improved, high death rates and epidemics prevailed for many years.

The pre-elementary school teacher should know these and other facts concerning the prevention of disease. However, they should not be presented to the children as isolated facts, to be learned by rote; rather, the prevention of disease should be taught through sessions on cleanliness, illness, and personal health. These topics should be discussed two or three times per week, and in a way which does not alarm the children.

ACCIDENTS

The pre-elementary school child should be taught to obey simple rules in the classroom, in the halls, and on the playground. However, interest overrides judgement in the pre-elementary school child, and the teacher must be alert to his actions so that accidents can be prevented. On the school playground, it is not unusual to see a child prepare to jump from a high box or platform without understanding that he will hurt himself in doing so. Whenever a child's safety is threatened, the teacher must be strict in enforcing rules.

ALARMS AND OFFERS

During the pre-elementary school program the child should develop the abilities to walk up and down stairs, and respond to a fire alarm. The school should teach him to refuse offers of candy, money, toys, and rides from strangers. He needs to learn to handle play equipment and toys carefully, to walk on the sidewalk, cross at corners, look both ways before crossing, obey all traffic signals, and not dart between parked cars.

BACKGROUND OF CHILD

Since the teaching of health and safety to the pre-elementary school child depends on the economic background and individual needs, it seems it would be wise to consider the characteristics of the child. By now, he has fairly well-developed muscles and is very active. He likes to learn new games, jump far, and climb high. He needs to be kept constantly busy with short periods of active play and frequent changes of activities because he has a short attention span and cannot sit quietly except for very short periods. Also, he has incomplete small muscle coordination, incomplete eye development, relatively small lungs, rapidly growing heart, and has begun losing teeth.

TRAINING IN HABITS

The child may be highly susceptible to fatigue, colds, common childhood diseases, and may have a tendency to revert to baby ways with thumb-sucking and baby talk. He is a poor loser, has difficulty making decisions and taking turns, and is greatly disturbed when confronted with disapproval. The child should also be becoming more self-dependent and able to accept responsibility, but he needs training in habits of personal hygiene and safety.

LOCOMOTION

The fundamental movements in locomotor and axial skills should be taught. These include walking, running, jumping, gliding, skipping, leaping, bending, turning, pulling, shaking, stretching, whirling, pushing, bouncing, rising, and swaying. Games using the activities of handling a ball, rolling, pushing, throwing, catching, and kicking, should also be taught.

IN THE HOME

The teaching of health and safety should begin in the home. Since much of this usually is lacking in the depressed areas, the school, then, has the responsibility for this teaching at the pre-elementary school level. Most of the instruction, however, can be taught through play and exercise activities.

REFERENCES

Piaget, J.: *The Construction of Reality in the Child* (translated by Margaret Cook). New York, Basic Books, 1954.

Chapter 9

ART

Many educators state that if all children had the same environment, there would be no difference in the rate of their development—and no special attention to stimulation of creative endeavor would be necessary. This would be a utopian society and every child could use his creativeness without resorting to an, "I cannot do that" attitude. He would not fear failure.

Unfortunately, such is not the case, and it is necessary to provide many children with special stimulation if they are to be creative. The inclusion of art as an integral part of pre-elementary schools can result in very meaningful experiences for young children.

A generalized developmental curve of creative thinking abilities of American children indicates that creative thinking begins at age three, peaks at about age five, and begins to decline at age five-and-a-half—right after many children enter pre-elementary school programs. This suggests the need for emphasizing means whereby the transition from home to school must be made, and the creativeness of the youngsters must be extended and presented by the new environment.

The child's interaction with his environment is creative in nature. He must respond in some way to the outside world. His responses become more complex, learning takes place and behavior changes. The schools should promote creativity—not stifle it.

Art is one way of overcoming environmental influences which have played a vital role in forming his personality. These activities, which require him to react, make decisions, reach judgments, and develop associations, provide a means for self-expression and a way to release frustration and hostility. For pre-elementary school children, art is good for the overall well-being of the "total child." It can touch his many human facets—including emotional, social, mental, and physical development.

EMOTIONAL SATISFACTION

Artistic production can enhance stability because it gives a child a way to express himself that is not verbal. This release offers the child a chance for creative expression. It appears that transition from kindergarten to first grade often stifles creative growth. Our lock-step system of education is partly to blame. Art activity, though, might be a means for reversing the tendency. The use of art as therapy for mental illness has long been established. The unconscious segment of a personality appears quite often through art expression and the interpretation of this, coupled with therapy, helps to restore a shattered personality. Thus, strengthening the artistic segment of personality serves as a preventive device.

Authorities say that children express their feelings more freely when easel-painting, than when using crayons. In crayon drawings, children seem to be more aware of the outside world and use the crayon media as a means of communication with other people, rather than as an emotional expression. Easel paints would be tempera paints in the primary colors of red, yellow, and blue, and perhaps the secondary color, green. If crayons are to be used, the larger ones are recommended.

SOCIAL DEVELOPMENT

As a social influence, art education is important because children are learning social skills when they share materials, observe others, or take turns with supplies. The fact that they are trying to master a skill enhances their social status. Children like to draw, and artistic activities such as drawing and painting help build body concepts and image.

Pre-elementary school programs should include an appreciation of beauty, for the sake of pleasure, as well as social development, and the physical environment of the classroom is one prime source. Color, design, and spatial relationships of the equipment in the room can be utilized to create a bright, colorful, but not cluttered atmosphere which can contribute to a child's feeling of beauty versus ugliness, and help motivate learning. During class, the painting of a tree can be utilized to depict the seasons of the year, while the session itself can be used to explain both nature and the nature of the environment.

PHYSICAL GROWTH

The teacher in the pre-elementary school can promote physical prowess by encouraging the use of large and small muscle activity. This can be done by assembling large blocks and having the student put them together in art forms, or by instructing the student in the art of finger-painting on large paper, or painting with clear water on a dusty chalkboard, hammering nails in a design, sawing styrofoam for a construction activity, or by drawing in the sand. All the activities just mentioned encourage motor development, as well as being artistic crafts. The fine motor skills in hand-eye coordination activities can be encouraged by the use of crayons, chalk, pencils, or ball-point pens for free drawing periods.

PERCEPTUAL TRAINING

A trend that is now established in pre-elementary school education stresses the training of perceptual awareness. This trend, based on work by Piaget, proposes that intelligence is developmental, and that perceptual development is the foundation of later abstract skills. This approach gives further credit to a great amount of art work with pre-elementary school children and states that this art work encourages intellectual and mental development.

Knowledge is based on information which we receive through sensory and perceptual processes. Art, then, is mainly an education of our senses. Art education would be perceptual training in that it teaches visual perception and visual discrimination through manipulation of materials. One interesting exercise for a teacher at the pre-elementary school level is to have the child smell a certain thing, then draw what he smells. In other words, his drawing would depict what this smell means to him. This is not only interesting but informative, particularly when a teacher differentiates between various smells and has the child draw what many things smell like to him. This often becomes fun to the students in the classroom and promotes both conversation and a great deal of fun.

The teacher can have the children learn about size and shape through art and spatial relationship activities. For example, the teacher can show the students similar objects of various sizes, and then say,

"Draw them." This is teaching spatial relationships as far as size and shape is concerned. We find shapes basic to all humanity in the art productions such as circles, squares, triangles, rectangles, etc.

Color is said to be the charmer of all mankind—and it is certainly the cornerstone of artistic endeavor. During the pre-elementary school years, it is practical for the teacher to use meaningful art activities whereby the child can become acquainted with color's existence, its characteristics, and with the feelings that various colors evoke in him. Any child can experience the use of color to express feelings which he cannot verbalize. Likewise, the idea of verbalization can be much enhanced while working with clay, or through measuring amounts of paints to be used.

Our culture is based primarily on verbal communication, but many children do not learn to verbally commit themselves. This is particularly true of the culturally deprived child who is often deficient in the facility to communicate with persons from different social backgrounds. However, all children can express themselves in art although their language may be poorly devised. We know that language development is one of the prime goals for training disadvantaged pre-elementary school children. This training can be enhanced considerably by art and other related activities.

Each child who explains his creation of art has an opportunity for verbalization. Young children create things that have meaning only to them, and they should be encouraged to share this with their classmates. They also should be allowed to just dabble with paint and express themselves by not making a picture of any significance. Art is a language because, as art therapy indicates, it serves as a means of communication. It enhances human relationships and should be used as a tool for language development.

Through art, the child quickly becomes curious and perceives much. He can learn to make significant choices and exercise much independent thinking as he learns to solve problems by exploring and experimenting in art activities. He develops an awareness of things around him by being involved. Many abstract processes are called into play through the organization of art activities, and through the decisions made in producing art crafts. The language of art, then, enables each child to gain knowledge, and to improve himself. It is also a good therapy.

As the child becomes more sensitive to his environment through art, he also becomes more aware of the essential quality of things. For example, he can be taught the four seasons of the year by drawing them. Discussions can be held concerning Christmas, Thanksgiving, and Halloween because the child has drawn things concerning these holidays. These pictures should be displayed on the walls around the room in order to foster group discussion. If a child draws a picture of an apple tree, then the entire group should discuss it. Perhaps the teacher could bring to class an apple with the stem still in it, and explain that the apple grows by its stem, hangs down until it becomes ripe, then the stem lets go and the apple falls from the tree.

It is true that disadvantaged children lack the motivation and initiative when it comes to art, but this is because they have not been given the opportunities for art activities at home. This is why it is necessary for them to have the opportunity to dabble and play in paints, draw with crayons or their fingers, and express themselves the way they have never been able to before. This is creativity, and every day that the child is given the opportunity to be creative, he will have a greater interexpression—and in all probability the hostility and frustrations usually kept within will be released through art activities.

Somewhere along the line, creativity in children is stifled. The author would hope it is not at the pre-elementary school level. It does appear to be somewhere between the first and second grades. Why this is true is not totally known, but the lock-step system of our educational process has a lot to do with it. It is true that perhaps we cannot overcome this lock-step system through pre-elementary school programs, but certainly, in an unstructured situation, we could go a long way in our art activities in promoting, rather than stifling, creativity.

Art education programs should be rich in environmental stimuli even though, in all probability, the children register only one thing at a time. The teacher of art in the pre-elementary school program needs to consider, and should strive to follow, the theories of learning which are taught in all colleges. In this way, the teacher can utilize art to teach at least a thousand other things—and art becomes a motivating factor and means of expression.

EXPRESSION

Expressions tend to develop systematically in children, and this occurs at various ages, thereby providing an opportunity for development in a humanistic way. The teachers of pre-elementary school children should know the developmental sequences because they are clues to what to look for at the next junction. This is particularly important for culturally disadvantaged children because research indicates they lag behind other children in visual motor development. Knowing this, the teacher can then use art in order to encourage the maturation process concerning visual motor development.

At about the age of two, the child begins to get around. He can hold a tool in his hand and even aim it at a target. He begins to make his first "scribbles" at about the age of two-and-a-half, and these first "scribbles" can be said to be the development of the language of art. We can compare this to the babbling stage in verbal language development and say that these "scribbles" are the end of the babbling stage, and that the child is ready to imitate. While he is making these "scribbles," he imitates, makes all kinds of markings, looks at them and feels a joy of accomplishment.

The lever-like makeup of the arm, wrist, and hand determines the child's movements, and one of the favorite patterns consists of arc-like marks all over the paper. The child also tends to use only about two-thirds of the paper when he is two-and-a-half or three years old, and whatever the culture, children seem to follow this developmental sequence. As the movements increase, children tend to use more of the paper, and the arc-like marks tend to get larger. This happens at a little past three years of age, and the child is then ready to go further into art activities. At this point in life, he should be shown different pictures of animals, and his parents should draw the animals, indicating to the child how much fun drawing really is. The child is perceiving spontaneously at the age of three and the circles become a black mask of pencil marks as the hand, wrist, and arm move around and around in an arc-like circle. After the child has mastered this, he is ready to move on to other shapes.

At about the age of four, the child moves into a stage of drawing shapes. Some shapes are definable, but most are not—as far as being able to look at them and tell exactly what they are. The shapes do

have meaning for the child, though, and parents and teachers alike
should be warned not to make fun of these drawings. One of the favorite designs which appears and prevails in children's art at this time is
the mandala—a design of perfect balance. The sun with the radials
reaching out from the circle is an example of the mandala. At this
age, children seem to love to draw the sun with the radials reaching
out.

At about the age of four-and-a-half, most children begin to draw
people. The circle is a man and the limbs extend from the circle. As
long as children draw naturally, the balance is an important feature
in their design. At this point, it should be noted that the drawings of
children indicate their intelligence. The more details that a young
child puts into a drawing, the more intelligent he is. For example, if
a four-and-a-half-year-old child puts eyebrows, eyelashes, eyes, lips and
nostrils in two dimensions on a human figure, then this would indicate
he is well-above average intelligence.

Most children become interested in drawing animals at the age of
five or five-and-a-half. Often, the animals are man-like creatures with
ears added. At this time, parents and teachers can be very helpful by
encouraging the child not only to draw animals, but to make up stories
about the animals they have drawn.

Children will draw when they are ready, and as stated earlier, this
is a part of the maturation of the child. Trying to get him to draw
when he is not ready is a futile effort. Children reach a point of want-
ing to tell about their world. When this happens, they begin to draw
people, houses, trees, and things about them. This usually happens
at about the age of six and suggests there must be a creative thrust in
the children concerning nature. This, too, should be encouraged, and
children should be asked to make up stories about things in nature they
draw.

At about the time they start drawing nature scenes, the art of children becomes pictorial. As already pointed out, the pre-elementary
school years are critical ones for child art. Therefore, a child should
feel free to use colors and basic shapes which please him. This should
be stated again and again in all books written about art in the pre-
elementary school years. The teacher should encourage the child to
utilize art for his pleasure—not for that of his parents or teacher. If

this happens, his love of art will continue to unfold and he will derive a great deal of satisfaction from it. The more structured the situation, though—in pre-elementary schools or even in the elementary years— the more likely the child is to have his creativity squashed.

We assume in America that art education for pre-elementary school children will neither expect too much of him nor take up too much of his time. While it is true that we should not expect more of the child than he can do, we should let him utilize his time in art to a great extent if he so desires. We should not have a regimented fifteen-minute art period, wherein all the materials are passed out by little children in the pre-elementary school room and then, at a certain time, all the materials are taken up. This only helps to stifle the love of art and creativity.

It has been found that the lag in art of disadvantaged children is very closely paralleled to their lag in other school subjects. Therefore, we can teach the disadvantaged children not only to enjoy art, but to do a better job in other areas, such as reading. Naturally, we do not have to teach a child to express himself through art. We are not trying to make artists of young children. However, we are trying to let them express themselves, have a good time, and use art in a pleasant learning situation.

There is no doubt that art is fun for young children. There is no doubt that young children spontaneously seek and enjoy artistic endeavors. There is no doubt that a structured program will stifle the ingenuity of these children. Knowing these things, why do so many schools try to put every subject and recreation area in small categories? For example, fifteen minutes for this, fifteen minutes for that, etc. What harm could possibly come from running five or ten minutes into the reading time if a child has a spark of creativity going and would like to finish?

We can do much for our young children by utilizing art. It is also true that we can stifle creativity through art exercises if we do them in the wrong way. A teacher should be cognizant of all the things mentioned in this chapter because, at this tender age, we have the child in a vulnerable position. We can do much that is constructive, but also much that can do great harm. In the pre-elementary school years, we should always strive to do the constructive things.

Chapter 10

COMMUNICATION

IN THE TERMS OF THE LAYMAN, "communication" should be thought of as the use of words and other symbols to transmit meanings from one person to others. The various skills used in communication we call "language arts." The language arts are an integral part of every person's daily activities and influence his entire life. Developing adequate communication skills involves learning to listen, speak, read, and write, in this order.

In college reading courses, we teach that listening and speaking make up the foundation for reading and writing by adding a wealth of background material for printed and written symbols. Before learning to read and write, the child must cultivate an inner language, and also develop an adequate self-image and awareness of things in his environment. Every person develops a mental picture of himself, and the picture should be a good one. The quality of this picture is determined by our experiences. Therefore, we must begin as early as possible to improve the self-image of the deprived, pre-elementary school child, even though it will be extremely difficult to change the family environment.

Before 1960, education for the deprived individual was focused mainly on programs for dropouts and remedial work in the inner-city schools. In the early sixties educators began to see that such programs were coming too late in the child's life, and that pre-elementary school education programs are essential for all children, but particularly for the culturally disadvantaged. By the age of three, the disadvantaged child is seriously behind other children in his development of aptitudes necessary for his success in first grade.

The parents' use of language has a great deal of influence on the speech of the child. Oral language becomes almost habitual in the child at a very early age. Studies indicate there is generally very little change after the age of three in the parts of speech used by a child, and that the greatest growth in articulation takes place between the ages of three and four.

The culturally disadvantaged child, in most cases, possesses a lower level of cognitive thinking ability than does the child from a higher socioeconomic home. The disadvantaged child tends to develop poor language skills, and to have a small vocabulary. He often does not know the names of familiar objects and seems to be uncertain of his own identity. The disadvantaged, pre-elementary school child may lack the ability to use language adequately enough to acquire information necessary for learning. He has not heard proper language in the home. Therefore, he is retarded in language development.

The linguistic style for the culturally deprived child is determined by his environment. Therefore, he has difficulty in ordering sequences deriving meanings and putting words into context. Although he listens, this child may miss much, since he has had limited experiences in his home environment. It should be pointed out though that in relation to his experiences, the culturally deprived child can be extremely verbal in his language.

The deprived child is slow in developing his language skills. A culturally disadvantaged child takes about a year longer to develop speech than does the advantaged child. These skills necessary for full-fledged communication are achieved at about seven years of age for the privileged child, and at about eight years of age for the deprived child. The low-status child displays more errors in language usage than other children because he has used his parents and siblings as "language models."

Society encourages proper language development in the child from the high socioeconomic level, while the child from the low socioeconomic home receives little encouragement. An effective person is so socially mobile in his use of language that the listener is more concerned with what he is saying than how he is saying it. Research indicates that an adult will spend at least 90 percent more of his time expressing his thoughts orally, than he will in writing (Webster, 1966). Therefore, it appears important to place a great deal of emphasis on improving the disadvantaged child's oral communication skills, as opposed to his writing skills. The teacher of the young deprived child must be familiar with activities and techniques to help guide him toward a better understanding and use of the language skills.

Some have said that a child learns first from life, and later from books. This is true. Research demonstrates that oral language growth is of utmost importance before reading instruction begins. The child from the middle and high status home usually receives enough daily experiences, love and attention to render him capable of learning— before reading instruction begins. This child customarily has exposure to people, animals, natural phenomena, the business world, explanations from parents, and the concepts of right and wrong. The disadvantaged child is usually found lacking in all the experiences mentioned above.

The skills required in learning reading, writing, and arithmetic are based on experiences. Experience, of course, is the foundation of later abstract learning, and hence, reading, writing, and arithmetic are symbols of thought and experience. Just because a child is taught to recognize words, he does not necessarily become a good reader. Word-calling without comprehension is of little value. He must acquire the skill of recognition to understand the ideas that are represented by the symbols. To enable the child to do this, he must have many experiences, and he must have the opportunity to encounter many situations in the first five or six years of life.

By age four or five, a child still has developed neither the proper eye-hand coordination nor the patience to sit still very long. His pre-elementary school activities should be geared toward providing the experiences which will lead to the learning of reading, writing, and arithmetic—formal instruction in these subjects coming later in life.

In the preceding passages we have applied the principle of developing speech, before that of reading and writing, to the culturally disadvantaged child. However, it is also important to apply it to the child from the culturally advantaged home. The failure to develop an oral vocabulary and an easy flow of expression in the child, prior to formal reading and writing instruction, results in the child failing to accomplish this very difficult tool proficiency.

The teacher in the pre-elementary school must endeavor to improve the communication skills of both disadvantaged and advantaged children. In doing this, she must first teach all the children to listen. It is extremely important to remember that although the disadvantaged child is severely handicapped in situations involving listening, it is possible that the advantaged child has not learned to listen. The attention span of any child may be short, and any child may lack proper auditory discrimination skills, and sufficient experiences to understand what he hears. He also may be easily distracted, and physically and socially immature. Exercises in listening to stories, poetry, and jingles published in various books and workbooks should be utilized by the pre-elementary school teacher in teaching listening skills.

The child gains most of his vocabulary, ideas, sentence patterns, and word structures by listening. It follows, then, that there are many ways in which a child listens. They enjoy hearing stories, poems, and music. The child must learn to listen to directions and announcements, and to understand what they are saying. Analytical listening, then, occurs when the child analyzes what he hears in terms of his own experience. If, after analyzing it, he fully understands, then we say he has developed adequate listening skills.

The disadvantaged child needs special help in developing these and other types of listening. However, many advantaged children also need help in developing these and other types of listening. Also, many children from advantaged homes are exceptional—they may have hearing losses, vision problems, mental retardation or special learning disabilities. It is also true that children from advantaged homes may have crippling conditions or chronic health disorders. There are many, many ways that children from advantaged homes can be handicapped, and these naturally can interfere with their learning ability.

The teacher should plan short periods of any one activity when a child has a very short attention span. In addition, the method of presentation should be varied because the child with a short attention span, or the hyperactive child, will get bored with the same type presentation. It is a known fact that when we vary our procedures, we hold the attention of the children better. This is also true with adults when we listen to a lecture or other type presentation—we are more likely to retain interest if the speaker varies his presentation from day to day rather than presenting it each time in the same old way.

The teacher should permit the child to wiggle and twist in his seat. This is contrary to what many people say, but it should be stressed that children are not young adults—they are children. They will wiggle in their seats and get nervous while sitting for long periods of time.

This is good—it would be too bad if they were to act other than like children. The child is too young to control his body movements in the pre-elementary school years and cannot sit still for a long length of time. Knowing this, why would any teacher demand that children do this? The child should feel comfortable in his seat, and outside noises and distractions kept to a minimum.

Do not repeat explanations or directions over and over. This gives the child too much of a crutch on which to lean. He must learn to be more than just a marginal listener. He must be a good listener.

A teacher should also strive not to talk too much. When the teacher talks too much, the children tend not to listen. If the children know that when the teacher says something, it is important, then they are more apt to listen.

The teacher at the pre-elementary school level should create a relaxed, happy atmosphere, and a good relationship with the child. The teacher, by all means, should pay attention to each child and remember that he or she is hungry for love and attention, whether advantaged or disadvantaged.

Help the child develop an awareness of sound, and begin by calling attention to sounds in the everyday environment. Teach the concepts of loud and soft, close and far away, sharp and dull, and other pertinent things dealing with sounds in everyday life.

We know that speech is a basic tool of communication, and that the child's family and peers are his first speech teachers. He imitates his mother and father, sisters and brothers, and other people in his immediate environment. The advantaged child has better models than the disadvantaged child and, therefore, has fewer problems. We know the disadvantaged child generally has poor language models, is often afraid to speak up in the classroom, and often seems to be unaware of what is going on.

The teacher's role in improving the oral communication of the disadvantaged child is not an easy task, in that the child has three kinds of problems with which to cope—his peers, his family, and his teacher. When he starts imitating his teacher and goes home in the afternoon using new words, there is a possibility that his family will make fun of him. When he comes back to school and uses the language of the home, there is a chance the children in the school will make fun of him. Naturally, no teacher should ever make fun of a child, but he does have a problem when he wants to imitate the teacher, yet feels that his words will not be accepted at home.

Speech that is learned later becomes a habit. If it is learned correctly when the child is young, then the habit is a good one. However, if poor speech patterns are developed, then the habit is a bad one. We all know that it is extremely difficult to break a bad habit. Certainly, it would be much better if all children had good examples to follow, and never developed bad speech habits. Unfortunately, this can not be, but if we can get these youngsters in pre-elementary school situations and bombard them with good speech of other people, then we have gone a long way in overcoming a bad habit before it actually becomes entrenched.

The pity is that we get too few of these children in pre-elementary school. As mentioned earlier in this book, we tend to do things backwards in American preschool education. The children whose parents can afford to send them to pre-elementary schools are generally not the ones who need it, and the parents who cannot afford to send their children to pre-elementary school are the ones who desperately need it. Until we change this situation, we are going to have thousands of children entering first grade every year who are far behind their peers in all areas of development.

The pre-elementary, disadvantaged child needs many and varied experiences—not only in listening, but in oral participation activities. He should be encouraged to speak, tell stories, and be in dramas in order that the teacher may hear his speech patterns and gently correct him if they are wrong. All children should participate in storytelling experiences and, if possible, note the errors that other children are making. In that few of them may be able to write, the teacher should gently point out these errors in a way that will not embarrass anyone. The important thing to be stressed here is that the child should have the opportunity to speak whereby others can hear and point out his errors. He then can hear how the words should be spoken when the others say them correctly.

REFERENCE

Webster, S. W.: *Educating the Disadvantaged Learner.* San Francisco, Chandler, 1966.

Chapter 11

SOCIAL LIVING

A NEW WORLD

W<small>HEN A CHILD</small> enters a pre-elementary school program, a whole new world begins for him because this type of social gathering is completely different from anything he has known. He encounters other children his age, and a teacher who is concerned about him and his family. He sees fat and thin, tall and short, blond and dark, quiet and rowdy—all types of children. He discovers that these children belong to his group, that they have privileges and rights, and that he must learn to deal with them while expressing his own feelings, if he wants to become an integral part of the group. He must get along with other children and the teacher in order to be liked and respected by all. Providing children the opportunity to learn basic essentials at this early stage will, in later life, help them to become contributors rather than parasites.

We hear a lot about various occupations which demand unskilled and semiskilled labor, and we know that the jobs in these areas are declining. Those jobs which require highly skilled labor are increasing rapidly. Children who become alienated from school, fail, and drop out do not achieve those skills required by a highly technical job field. Therefore, as children prepare for future jobs, they must master social amenities if they are to achieve self-respect, be able to identify with others, be motivated to achieve, and develop the desire to possess the intellectual abilities to cope with the changing needs of our social system. Usually, culturally disadvantaged children have difficulty in assuming a competent and satisfying life in the American picture because they do not have the opportunity to develop those skills which are needed for success.

NAMES AND NUMBERS

Pre-elementary school children must be able to tell their names and age, whether their families have a telephone, and know the difference between what belongs to them and what belongs to others. However, we must realize that many disadvantaged children have never even had to tell anyone their name, age or address. Because so many disadvantaged children come from cramped living quarters where no emphasis is placed on an individual's possessions, programs must provide them the opportunity to learn this concept. This is as much a part of life as knowing one's phone number.

The social life of pre-elementary school programs should provide for various social contacts and experiences. Good social experiences often come through situations which involve play, individual rights, the development of conversational skills and abilities, and knowing one's social limits. A teacher can be a vital force in promoting the child's confidence in himself, and in encouraging him to realize his potential so he may grow in social interactions and build an adequate self-image.

FAIR PLAY

A teacher should take a definite role in promoting fair play experiences among children because this is the first authoritative play they have had. A teacher's role is to act as guide when the rights of certain children are threatened. While doing this, the teacher must often search for underlying reasons for children's behavior.

In daily associations with children, the teacher can help them understand and accept the principles of fair play. This is done by rules and regulations, by using situational opportunities, and by the children and teacher planning organized activities together. In this way, the child learns the principles of fair play and practices them while using experiences which he, the other children, and the teacher have planned. It is extremely important to remember that the standards of fair play are constantly conveyed through the teacher's own conduct, and that children tend to follow the teacher example. The teacher must be an excellent model.

In many cases, disadvantaged children have been forced to rely on themselves to get what they want. Therefore, their initial activities in a pre-elementary school program may be overly aggressive and indicate a great deal of ego involvement. Teachers will probably have to be very firm.

The teacher should allow the children to work out their own problems whenever possible. However, the teacher must also indicate a definite interest when they have fights and other conflicts. The disadvantaged child probably may not have had the experience of talking out his problems. He may have been ignored or simply left out of any adult conversation because his problems did not seem important to his parents, or because his parents did not recognize problems. When given the chance to discuss their problems, children learn to use language as a means of resolving conflicts. This is a type of therapy and naturally, a mode of inner-expression.

Learning to express one's individual rights in a socially acceptable manner begins early and lasts throughout life. The atmosphere of pre-elementary school programs should encourage this expression of individual rights. Because many disadvantaged children have never experienced having their rights recognized and accepted, they must be given this freedom. However, they must learn not to deprive others of opportunities of self-expression, or to let their own expression interfere with the group. Teachers can help children express their individual rights by encouraging them to make choices, helping each one feel he is an important member of the group, and by encouraging everyone to respect each other's opinion.

One of the most basic social values in the education of the young disadvantaged child is learning to share materials, responsibilities, and space. Naturally, the sharing of responsibilities and experiences should be varied and continuous in order to hold each child's interest. Responsibilities in the classroom, such as emptying the wastebasket and handing out paper and pencils, should be divided up and rotated. This is a must to the learning of how to share community responsibilities. Since space in pre-elementary school programs may be limited, it is necessary that children learn to share space and get along in a limited area. Children must also learn that different persons have different mental and physical abilities, and that each one can contribute to the classroom according to his ability.

Any young child, average or disadvantaged, must be taught the fundamentals of courtesy. Such things as listening when others are talking, limiting activities when they interfere with the rights of others, learning to understand and appreciate the efforts and accomplishments of others, and learning to give and accept criticism are necessary for success in dealing with people throughout one's life.

There are several different ways a teacher can contribute to a child's social growth. If a child cries, he is often looking for adult support. In such a case, the teacher can do a couple of things: She can (1) stimulate sharing by making suggestions rather than posting rules and regulations; (2) offer the child experiences which evoke positive and constructive social responses in a natural, easy flowing way.

One of the pre-elementary school's most important contributions is to help children acquire techniques and skills. If the children have developed self-respect and a sense of worth, they will feel this way about other children also, and will acquire skills and techniques which improve overall relationships. Children will, however, continue to need help from adults. The teacher is more effective if she views herself as a valuable person and functions in terms of an adequate and capable individual. The children can learn truly and comfortably the tasks and joys of social living if the teacher is capable and has a feeling of adequacy.

Concerning the social living in the pre-elementary schools in America, it should be noted that we are oriented in a backward manner. The children who are able to afford pre-elementary school programs are the very ones who generally do not need it. They are the advantaged children. In most nursery schools and kindergartens, the child (i.e., the parent) is required to pay from fifteen to fifty dollars per month. The people who can afford to send their children to these schools are the ones who have advantaged homes, books in the homes, good food, television, and they also read and talk to their children.

The children who should be going to these nursery schools and kindergartens are the disadvantaged children whose parents cannot afford to send them. Consequently, when they enter the first grade, the disadvantaged children are approximately three years behind their middle class counterparts in social adjustment. This does not seem to be changing in America, and a gloomy picture prevails concerning the disadvantaged child in pre-elementary school education unless something is done immediately.

Social living is a very important part in the lives of both advantaged and disadvantaged children. The children who got to interact with their peers and other adults not in their socioeconomic level are the ones who will do better in academic subjects and social adjustment during the first few years of school. The ones who miss this social interaction start behind the others, and get further behind during the elementary school years. After about six years of this, the child is totally lost in the mire and is never ever able to catch up academically or socially.

It should be noted here that millions of Americans seem unwilling to support free pre-elementary school education for all children. This is said because so many states in 1971 do not have mandatory legislation for pre-elementary school education. Until all 50 states in America have mandatory pre-elementary school education for all children, the disadvantaged child will continue to be discriminated against, will be poorly adjusted in the elementary school years, and will not be able to function at his potential level.

Many states are doing an excellent job for all children at the pre-elementary school level. These states are to be commended for a job well-done, but Americans should not stop there. They should ask for legislation through federal and state governments for all children in pre-elementary school education, and in all parts of America— urban and rural sections alike.

The social life of any individual is important, and this life begins the day that a person is born. If this important segment of a person can be augmented during the early years, if he can be introduced to things foreign to him, and if he can learn what other people are doing, then he will begin first grade ready and eager to learn the things he must learn to compete in our modern society.

Chapter 12

MUSIC IN THE PRE-ELEMENTARY SCHOOL

Music is a very important factor in man's development, and has the power to unite and solidify groups ranging from the family to the people in the community. Since music is a universal means of communication, the variety of experiences which it can communicate is extremely diversified and virtually unlimited. It is because of this that music should become a major part of the educational program of pre-elementary school programs.

Music is an emotional experience. Therefore, its content can be varied—as can all other human emotions. Very often, the way an individual feels is more important to him than the way he thinks. If this is true of the adult, then it must also be true for children. A happy child is happy because he spontaneously feels happy, and not because he knows the definition of happiness. A child may be able to learn and think logically, but it is the way he feels about what he has learned that determines what he does with his knowledge. It is a known truth that children do well those things which they want to do, thereby making "want" an emotional condition.

Effective teaching requires a teacher to know each one of her pupils. In order to understand one child, the teacher needs to know the general characteristics of children in a particular age group, with specific attention being paid to how they interact with one another, and to each other. She must also realize that no one list of general characteristics will apply to all children in a particular age group. Also, it can not be assumed that certain characteristics will always be found at a specific age level. Certain characteristics will appear earlier for some children and later for others. This is especially true of the child from lower socioeconomic levels who tends to develop characteristics at a later age than an advantaged child does. No doubt, the knowledge of "norm" expectations is valuable in organizing a curriculum because it points out the deviations from the so-called average, and these differences can be used to identify the abilities or problems of children.

[121]

Experiences in music should be available to all children even though they will differ in musical talent, interests, etc. All children can learn to value and enjoy music regardless of special aptitudes (Lambert, 1958). Teaching of music, based on enjoyment and appreciation, is an excellent way to teach motor development, communication skills, cooperation, and self-expression. Also, music programs help teachers gain the children's interest—an absolute prerequisite for any instructional program.

A room forty by sixty feet is generally ample for most music programs. Chairs should be moved back against the wall to allow for freedom of movement. There should be ample space between the children in order for them to move freely.

The duration of the lesson need not be a full hour. A thirty-minute period, if well-planned, is usually sufficient—depending on the choice of the particular lesson and the readiness of the group.

Visual experience should be used in conjunction with the lesson, whenever possible, in order to convey the idea of the exercise to the youngsters. Visual experiences can take the form of movies, pictures, drawings, or real-life experiences. A good test as to whether or not children understand the lesson's theme is to allow them to draw the theme, discuss their drawings in small groups, and then with the entire group.

Readiness commands can be used to gain the attention of children before a lesson begins. For example, music may be played, the group may be told to form a circle, or certain commands such as "put your feet together" or "spread them apart" may be given. Ideally, the group should be small enough for the teacher to give individual attention to each child, and to let each child enjoy the others.

In teaching certain techniques to children, especially in attempting to coordinate body movements with music, it is necessary to demonstrate to the youngsters the value of proper movements. For example, the teacher can demonstrate the awkwardness of a movement by showing comically how silly feet pointed toward each other look, when compared with feet which are pointed properly.

The curriculum should be designed so the child can develop a healthy self-image, accept orientation for classroom situations, learn respect for other people, follow directions, and develop rapidly in academic readiness. The music program should be designed in such a way as to augment the total program. The child's senses should be exposed to music in some form as a means of encouraging him to listen, look, touch, feel, integrate and organize his thinking, communicate, and have fun.

The teaching of music must begin with simple things, and should be based on the group's social experience and development level. Naturally, this will vary, and each child should be considered in the music lesson.

The first aspect which should be taught is the body image, and this can be combined with motor coordination activities. The teacher may use a song which requires the children to name and point to different parts of the body, such as: "These are my eyes, and I have two. These are my ears, and I hear you. These are my lips, which move to talk—and I use my feet when I walk." In this procedure, the teacher says the song first, then sings it, and the children copy the action. In some cases, music may be added after motions have been learned.

The larger muscles of young children are better developed than the smaller ones. Therefore, in the beginning phase, physical activities involving the larger muscles should be stressed. Examples of such activities are walking, running, hopping, and even skipping. It is good to let the children become involved in the music by having them respond freely to recordings that "tell them what to do."

The language development of young children is limited, and speech skills are undeveloped. However, both language and speech growth can be rapid when stimulating experiences are provided. We should employ music to improve language and speech skills. The teacher should use chants, finger-play, singing games, and songs with words that are rhythmic, repetitious and even nonsensical.

Provisions should be made for creative responses to the sounds of words and music. Singing or chanting of nursery rhymes is good to use.

The teacher can help children who are shy and have trouble expressing their ideas and feelings, by encouraging them to listen and respond to music. This can be accomplished through dramatization of songs, or by having children imitate people and animals or other things. For example, the teacher may use a song about a bean growing. Before having the children imitate the growth of the bean, she could plant a real bean in a pot in the classroom, and explain to the children that the plant will sleep at first under the warm earth, and then wake and grow. The bean will get thirsty, so it will need water. She should further explain that, as the bean begins to grow, its leaves will stretch out toward the sun and eventually, a flower will form. Then, little beans will be produced which will eventually grow into big beans. The children can draw pictures of the bean's various phases of growth, and then imitate, in their own creative way, the growth which will take place. They could even make up a song about the bean and its growth. After the bean has actually grown, the children can compare the way they envisioned the growth of the bean with the way the bean actually grew. Photographs of various phases of the growth process should be taken and put on the bulletin board in sequential order.

Another important thing for pre-elementary school teachers to remember is that young children tend to be self-centered and involved. For this reason, each child should be allowed to sing by himself and both small and large groups, unless he is too shy. He will sing cooperatively in a large group when he is socially mature enough to participate in such a group. The teacher must set goals for group response in order for the children to learn cooperation in singing, taking turns, and listening to others. The teacher should create chants and conversational singing which include each child's first and last name. Short, repetitious songs are also fun, and acting is another good technique to use. All of the techniques are to be carried out without putting too much pressure on the child to remember words and tunes.

The teacher must be aware that young children have not developed the talent of staying in harmony. Therefore, emphasis should be placed on melody and rhythm, and later harmony will develop after practice and participation. Songs which require no chord changes should be used at first, and later harmonic changes can be included.

When singing, children enjoy the sounds of repetitious activities. Therefore, repetitive songs and motions with percussion instruments and bells may be included with great success. Music activities help children understand and appreciate others, and makes them aware of the quality of their word. Discussions and evaluations of music lessons help children communicate with, and relate to, other children.

Pre-elementary school children are inquisitive and eager to learn about, and respond to, their environment. The teacher needs to provide opportunities for these young children to use and experiment with a variety of musical materials and equipment. She should plan music experiences that build a respect for the beauty of melody, rhythm, form, and help them recognize the difference between happy, sad, slow, fast, high, and low. If possible, the children should be given the opportunity to experiment with various types of sounds obtainable from wood, metal, glass, stone, and various percussion instruments by introducing them one at a time. Naturally, all pre-elementary schools will not have these instruments available.

Children are interested in "today" more so than in the future. Songs about everyday experiences such as mother and father, playthings, the family, pets, etc., are excellent motivating devices for the teacher to use. The teacher must plan lessons which guarantee that every child will be given an opportunity for success. Music can be used as a "core" for learning. For example, a song concerning the American flag can be used to teach children about color and design.

The voices of children are not fully developed and many children need help in discovering their singing voices. Teachers may use tone-matching games, chants, or singing conversations to help the child find their singing voices. Children can be taught to listen and respond to pitches by vocally imitating sounds in their environments such as trains, whistles, church bells, and the sound of animals and machines. Also, they can imitate certain sounds in nature such as a whistling wind or a gurgling brook. Oral, aural, and visual aids are necessary in building pitch concepts.

The teacher must remember that one very important goal she is striving to accomplish is the building of a creative, spontaneous, and uninhibited action on the part of each child. The teacher should encourage the use of chants, interesting word-rhythms, rhythmic movement, and dramatizations to help reach the above-mentioned goal.

Commissioner McCurrin (1963) stated in an address:

> One of the major deficiencies in our national effort to meet the challenges before us is the almost complete failure of the American people

to recognize that the strength of a nation lies in its art and music and literature, and in its philosophical sophistication and the quality of its social sciences, just as much as in its physics and chemistry or its electrical engineering. When we raise the question of the survival of our nation, it is a question in proximate range of statesmanship and machinery. But when we speak of the decline or rise of our culture, and the strength of the nation for the long haul ahead, it is a question of the full cultivation of our spiritual, artistic, moral and intellectual resources. Those who suppose that great music, great poetry, or a knowledge of classical literature are not essential to either the quality or even the survival of a nation and its culture are quite unaware of the lessons of the past.

REFERENCES

Lambert, H. M.: *Teaching the Kindergarten Child.* New York, Harcourt, Brace and World, 1958.

McMurrin, C.: Report on special U.S. conference. *Washington Music Educator, 7*:30, 1962.

Chapter 13

LANGUAGE PROBLEMS IN THE FIRST FEW YEARS OF LIFE

THE CHILD'S LANGUAGE TRAINING begins the moment he hears a spoken word. This could be from nurses, parents, or people in the hospital, but it is not long until a child's language growth revolves around the home. Through the process of constant repetition, the child begins to associate certain words and sounds with the things that are in his environment. Some children are faster than others in these associations, and for some children it is a long drawn-out process. For most children, though, at a later date, after the association and repetition, the child attempts to reproduce words he has heard and gradually develops an understanding of language. Naturally, at a very young age, his understanding is limited to just a few words. But as these words and others are repeated over and over, the child gradually associates them with symbols.

Few parents realize that language, oral or written, forms the base of their child's education, and from this cornerstone of language skills rises the structure that later constitutes a modern education that most parents desire for their children.

By the time the child reaches the nursery or kindergarten, he has had language training for several years, has become an egocentric and self-centered person, and language provides a means by which he gets what he wants. In this egocentric speech, the child generally makes no attempt to address himself to a person. There is no particular problem when no one is listening because he talks for himself, or to himself, or to anyone who happens to be in hearing distance. To many adults, this represents immaturity, but this is not true. As previously stated, the child has been in training for several years for speech, and when he gets to this egocentric stage, he has passed several stages in language development.

During this egocentric stage, he finds that he gets attention and receives affection when he says certain things which please adults. At this point in the child's life, he has begun to recognize the value of interaction with people. Piaget (1926) discussed a second type of speech which he called socialized speech. In socialized speech, usually evident at seven or eight years of age, the child addresses himself to a particular person, considers the other person's point of view, and many actually exchange ideas with him.

When we consider that each person receives and interprets things in terms of his own experiences, then this self-centered vocalizing is not unique to the pre-elementary school child. To some degree, this self-centered approach to language is expected of people of all ages.

By the time a child starts elementary school, he has had many experiences which have helped to create a vocabulary of many, many words. He is generally eager to learn, and is full of experiences which he will openly discuss. The children in elementary school begin to hear, see, and feel new and interesting things. It is also true that they display firm language habits. These language habits have been learned over a period of several years, and they are extremely difficult to change if they are bad ones. It is also true that the correctness of these language habits is not questioned by the children. As a matter of fact, they think very little about speech and language habits, because they have learned them through imitation. If, at this early age—whether it is nursery school, kindergarten, or first grade—their faulty language habits are pointed out to them by other children in a noncomplimentary manner, of course an ego deflation can be expected. But to a child, if he can say something and the person to whom he is speaking can understand, then there is no language problem. But these initial language habits do become immediate to the elementary teacher, and to many of the children in the elementary school. This is particularly true because children are cruel. They will quickly point out flaws in other children, and are very quick to laugh at these flaws.

Many children fail in school primarily because their language is inferior. They first have to improve their language before they are ready to move on to the next step in the learning process. Therefore, they fall farther and farther behind. Perhaps in the future, if these inferior habits are detected at the pre-elementary school ages, then an appropriate course of action can be taken so the child will not have to suffer the consequences of failure.

A simple solution to this dilemma, of course, would be early identification of children destined to be school failures. Equally important is a program for early training. However, a stamp indicating "inferior" should not be placed on the child.

If early training of these children takes place, ultimately there will be fewer special education classes. Furthermore, public money will no longer be spent trying to patch up weaknesses that should have been identified, assessed, and corrected before elementary school.

Bangs (1968) states that if early assessments are not made, the child attempts to protect himself from his inadequacies in a number of ways: he withdraws from his peer group and becomes engrossed with specific toys, or he is disobedient when requests are asked of him. According to the author, cutting through these compensatory mechanisms at the age of five or six is a much more difficult diagnosis, assessment, and training task, than it would have been at an earlier age.

Research indicates that in regards to language problems, the older a child is, the more difficult it is to correct them. The older child has already built up defense mechanisms, and these must be removed before even beginning to correct the basic problem.

THE THERAPIST

With this potpourri of information, it is evident that speech therapy is no simple matter. Volumes could be written on corrective techniques and methods for disorders. Time does not allow a comprehensive analysis of corrective measures for each disorder. However, this brief look at speech disorders in general gives us a better understanding of the many types of defects and difficulties that have befallen the speech therapist. Remarks will be restricted primarily to methods used in correction of articulatory errors—the ones most commonly found which are a favorite of speech therapists.

DIAGNOSIS AND EVALUATION

The two most commonly used terms referring to the presumed etiology or causation of articulatory errors are dyslalia and dysarthria. The first refers to disorders of functional origin where the cause may be due to mislearning, imitation, emotional conflicts, or the like. Dysarthria implies a disorder of articulation due to impairment of the part of the central nervous system which directly controls the muscles of articulation.

Defects in articulation constitute the bulk of speech disorders. Hundreds of surveys prove this. Much to the therapist's delight, articulatory cases respond most easily and quickly to therapy, but there are many exceptions to this rule.

Most parents want to begin immediately to correct a child who says, "whittle," instead of "little." They feel the child has made a mistake and should correct it. The speech therapist takes a different approach. He must come to grips with the problem. Like the detective or lawyer, he must get to the "facts." He attempts to answer the questions: "Why does the child have articulatory errors?" "What are the errors?" And finally, "What must be done to eliminate them?"

One of the first duties of the therapist in any thorough analysis is to consider the developmental factors. This is on the assumption that the child has been referred. He should explore the maturation of articulation in the child. This would come from parent interviews. All of the child's past history should be investigated to determine the origin of the problem. Any illness, accident, or abnormalities in growth could be significant. The child's hearing acuity and intelligence needs to be known. Also, it is helpful to know the amount of speech stimulation in the home, and the attitude of the parents toward the defect. Often the cause is lost somewhere in the midst of speech development. An earlier cause that was highly effective in contributing to the defect may have since subsided, while the defect persists. Then, too, there is the possibility of speech being mislearned. A child may habitually say "thoup" because of poor teaching. We also must not forget emotional factors, often important in cases of delayed speech. This preliminary investigation and history-taking is basic. Misdiagnosis is a curse to any true speech therapist.

Some parents believe their child has faulty articulation due to organic abnormalities. Misarranged teeth, swollen tonsils, and a shortened frenum (tongue-tie) are often suspected. However, speech therapists are usually conservative in attributing the defective sounds to organic factors. There is on record too many instances of good, intelligible speech where organic factors are present. There are those who have no teeth who can produce all the speech sounds correctly. There are individuals with no or half-a-tongue who speak intelligibly. It is possible to compensate. A perfectly good "L" sound may be produced with the tongue-tip down or even outside the mouth. The difference lies in the extra effect in learning to overcome these obstacles. This does not mean that the therapist should discount organic deviations entirely, but he should consider them important—along with the many other possible causes.

Modern surgery has done wonders in the reconstruction of dental, palatal, and jaw structures. Although most undertakings of this sort are tremendously expensive, it is the duty of the therapist to refer those with marked mouth deformities to these specialists. Especially in cases of severe organic defects in children, the therapist should convince the parents of the need for corrective measures. One way is to point out the social maladjustment which such defects may produce.

Another important factor in any satisfactory diagnosis is that the therapist should make a complete phonetic analysis of the individual's speech. This is vitally important for therapy. Van Riper (1963) gives three major objectives in making a phonetic analysis: Find (1) the sounds which are defective; (2) the type of error in terms of suberror within the word (initial, medical, or final). This gives us an idea what sound or sounds are defective, and how much ear training is needed. It helps the therapist better understand the scope of the problem. You ask, "What method do you use to find these errors?" Most therapists use a standard picture articulation test. For adults, special phonetically structured sentences are often used. One of the best is the Developmental Picture Articulation Test by Henja. The Bryngleson and Glaspey Picture Articulation Test is also widely used among speech therapists. The pictures are arranged in sequential order of the development of consonant sounds. They begin with the plosives (*p, b*) and run through the completion of blends like *s*led and um*b*rella. After gaining rapport with the child, he is asked to say aloud the pictures. On a scoring blank, the therapist records phonetically any misarticulated sound—whether it is at the beginning, middle, or end of a word. This is getting the child's errors down on paper so the therapist can see the problem in better perspective.

It is advantageous for the therapist to carry the evaluation a step further and get a kinetic analysis. It is not just enough to say a child has a lisp. We need to determine whether it is lateral, occluded, interdental, or nasal in the formation of the lisp. In short, the important thing is the manner of production. An attempt is made to find just what the child is doing when he makes an error. One method is for the therapist to imitate or duplicate what the child is doing. Each of the speech sounds may be incorrectly produced in several ways. For example, errors of stop-plosives such as "k" and "g" seem to be due to (1) the wrong location of the tongue contact; (2) the wrong speed in forming the contacts; and (3) the wrong structures used in contacts. A child who says "tandy" for "candy" is using a tongue-palatal contact, but it is too far forward. Too slow a release from a "k" contact may give a breathy, aspirate quality to the utterance. "Kuheep the kueys" is an example of this.

A common error is the use of the wrong channel for the airstream. This is seen when using an unvoiced "L" for the "S." Also, the airstream may be in the wrong direction as in the case of a nasal lisp. The "S" is inhaled. Too weak an air pressure may cause an omission of sounds.

The reproduction of the error enables the therapist to understand its nature. Only after careful analysis of the articulatory error and breaking of the old habit can the therapist begin any thorough sessions. Most progress can be made after the case understands clearly what he is doing wrong. Insight into error is a must before significant progress is to be made.

A final factor to be considered in an evaluation is the condition under which errors occur. We need to examine each error in terms of the following: (1) type of communicative situation, (2) speed of utterance, (3) kind of communicative material, and (4) discrimination ability. Some lispers only have difficulty when under emotional stress. Children may imitate correctly, but distort their own speech sounds. Knowing when a child makes his errors helps in the therapy.

At the end of the examination, all of the information is put together in a systematic and meaningful way. If the therapy plan is to be successful, the information gained must be organized. The following is a form commonly used:

CASE: AGE: GRADE: ADDRESS: PHONE:

Family history:
Developmental history:
Birth history:
Present physical conditions:
Behavior:
Type of disorder:
Phonetic errors:
Intelligence:
Hearing acuity:
Muscular coordination:
General observation of speech:

The therapist is now ready for therapy. Up until now, this chapter has described defects that would be corrected in individual therapy. For the most part, this will be the major concern of speech therapists. However, speech therapy can be accomplished by other methods. There are several approaches being used to reach and help those with speech handicaps. One could be referred to as a general speech improvement program. (Technically, this is not speech therapy per se.)

SPEECH PROBLEMS

Speech and the need to express ourselves adequately is of paramount importance in this most vocal of worlds. An agile tongue is to be envied. Oral speech forms the very core of our communication with our fellow peers. It is something upon which we rely practically every day of our lives. The ordinary business of life presents many opportunities for the use of oral communication. Not only is it a transmissive thing, but psychologists have shown that the ability to "think aloud" has become an economic necessity. We win and lose jobs, not on how little or how much we know, but rather on how well we are able to "sell" ourselves and our talents.

Obviously, then, there is a large responsibility on us as parents, teachers and specialists in the field of speech to see that every child has the opportunity to develop his speech skills to the fullest—a facility which our society so highly rewards both in school and in later life. Since these skills are a product of the learning process, it is only natural that many will fall by the wayside as the result of some hindrance. These latter ones will be the focal point of our discussion.

RECOGNIZING SPEECH DISORDERS

In order to correct speech defects, one must be able to recognize speech disorders. Let us consider, "What is a speech defect?" According to Van Riper (1963), speech is defective "when it deviates so far from the speech of other peope that it calls attention to itself, interferes with communication, or causes its possessor to be maladjusted." Condensing this somewhat, we might say that speech is defective when it is conspicuous, unintelligible or unpleasant.

Berry and Eisenson (1956), in their definition, include an additional subjective aspect. They propose that speech may be considered defective when the speaker becomes excessively self-conscious or apprehensive about objectively small deviations, or assumed deviation in his manner of speaking. In a broad sense, any speech deviation, however small, becomes a significant defect if it interferes with the speaker's social adjustment. We could sum it up in one sentence: Speech is defective when it deviates.

But who is to judge? The cultural norms of society really determine how deviate speech must be before it is conspicuous. For example, we would not consider a child of three who said "wabbit" for "rabbit" as having a speech defect. However, this certainly would be uncommon among adults. Defective speech is characterized in the following descriptions:

(1) not easily audible; (2) not readily intelligible; (3) vocally unpleasant; (4) deviates in respect to specific sound (consonant, vowel, or diphthong) production; (5) labored in production; (6) linguistically deficient; (7) inappropriate to the speaker in terms of age, sex, and physical development; (8) visibly unpleasant.

TYPES OF SPEECH DISORDERS

As one can easily see, it is apparent that much can be wrong with the manner in which an individual speaks. In fact, the range of defects is so wide that Van Riper (1963) has conveniently divided them into four categories: (1) articulation, (2) time (or rhythm), (3) voice, and (4) symbolization (language). It would help the reader understand the corrective techniques better if we review, briefly, speech disorders in general. For this, we will select one classification and describe corrective measures. It is far beyond the scope of this chapter to discuss them all.

ARTICULATION

Under disorders of articulation, we include all those disorders characterized by the substitution, omission, addition, and distortion of the speech sounds. A child who omits the "s" might say, "In the 'ummer, I like to 'wim, 'kate and ride my bi'ykle." One who adds on would say, "My umburella is bluack and grueen." There are several concomitant terms related to these disorders—namely, "baby talk," sometimes called infantile perseveration and characterized by sound substitutions during the early stages of child development; "lalling," which is due to the sluggishness of the tongue tip and characterized by defective "a, l, t, d, or s" sounds; "lisping," a (frequent) disorder of the "s" and "z" sounds; delayed speech; unintelligible consonants; and "oral inaccuracy," a general term for any mild articulatory defect. One must keep in mind that these defects do not always occur independently, but may appear jointly in an individual's speech. For example, a laller may also lisp, or one who lisps may talk baby talk.

Many people would tend to overlook articulatory defects as being serious. Some even think it is cute in children. Although most children outgrow their speech difficulties, there are many who do not. Of the 5 percent of children having serious speech defects, 3 percent have problems of articulation. One estimate states there are approximately 120,000 children of school-age who have functional articulatory defects (Berry and Eisenson, 1956). This figure justifies therapy. In working with speech defectives, the number of articulatory errors are sometimes so great that the speech is nothing more than an unintelligible jargon (idioglossia). Corrective procedures for articulatory errors will be discussed later.

TIME AND RHYTHM

The second major category of disorders is that of time and rhythm. We speak language in a sequential pattern—in that sound follows sound, syllable follows syllable. When something disrupts the spontaneous flow of speech to the degree that it is conspicuous, unpleasant, or unintelligible, we have a disorder of time. A prime example is the stutter. This disorder, which has affected men throughout the ages, ranks second under articulatory disorders. About 280,000 school-age children are gripped by this perplexing problem. An interesting thing about stuttering is that it seems to be more of a communicative disorder than one of speech. Most stutterers speak fluently when alone or singing. The impediment appears while under emotional stress or while confronted with others in a speaking situation.

There have been many books written on the subject, and presently, several theories are being considered as to the cause or causes. Johnson (1956), an authority in the field, claims that stuttering is a learned behavior having several stages. Others feel that stuttering is a symptom of phychoneurosis, or due to some physical difference. Early recognition and referral of a stutterer to a trained therapist is an excellent recommendation, for it may save much anxiety, frustration, and embarrassment in later years.

Cluttering is also a disorder of time or rhythm. Distinguished from stuttering, it is characterized by excessive speed in speaking, disorganized sentence structure, and slurred or omitted syllables and sounds.

VOICE

The third category of speech defects is that of voice disorders (dysphonia). As mentioned previously, the sounds of speech may be articulated incorrectly and the noises, sounds, and tones themselves may be less than one-half percent to more than one percent may have difficulties in vocalization (Johnson, 1956). Some of the possibilities for voice disorders are as follows: too-high pitch, too-low pitch, monotone, pitch breaks, and stereo-typed inflections (Van Riper, 1963). There may be disorders in voice intensity or loudness and voice quality. Examples might be voices that are too weak or too loud, hypernasal, strident, falsetto, breathy, or hoarse.

SYMBOLIZATION

The fourth category of disorders concerns problems of symbolic formulation and expression (dysphasia). Speech and all the language functions may be affected singly or jointly because of brain damage. Although these individuals comprise a small percentage of speech defectives, they are no less important. Aphasia is a handicap that is often difficult to diagnose. According to Wepman (1951), it may be one of two types: (1) inability to express ideas through spoken or written language symbols (expressive); (2) disturbance in the ability to comprehend language through spoken or written symbols (receptive).

Therapy for aphasics presents many frustrations and challenges for the speech therapist.

RELATED SPEECH DISORDERS

Mention must be made of other related speech disorders. There are those of cleft palate, foreign accent, deaf and hard-of-hearing speech, and cerebral palsy. These disorders do not always appear as distinctive entities. One might have a combination of several defects. Although these later ones mentioned compromise relatively small numbers, they, along with stuttering, present great difficulties in treatment.

REFERENCES

Bangs, T. E.: *Language and Learning Disorders of the Pre-Academic Child.* New York, Appleton Century Crofts, 1968.

Berry, Mildred and Eisenson, Jon: *Speech Disorders.* New York, Appleton Century Crofts, 1956.

Johnson, Wendell: *Stuttering in Children and Adults.* Minneapolis, University of Minnesota Press, 1956.

Piaget, J.: *The Language and Thought of the Child.* New York, Harcourt, Brace, 1926.

Van Riper, Charles: *Speech Correction Principles and Methods.* Englewood Cliffs, N.J., Prentice-Hall, 1963.

INDEX

A

Absenteeism, 5
Abstract problems, 12
Achievement level, 19
Administrator, 28
Adults, 30
Advantaged child, 111, 114
Alcoholism, 8
America, 12, 15, 49, 51, 60, 109
American
  children, 102
  education, 3, 9, 37
  preschool education, 115
  schools, 50
Americans, 120
Anxiety, 6, 136
Appalachian Mountains, 50
Arithmetic, 45, 63, 69, 70
Art, 14, 105
  activities, 107
  education, 104, 106
Articulation, 134, 135
Artistic production, 103
Atmosphere, 114
Auditory memory, 79
Auditory skills, 14
Average, 18
Axial skills, 101

B

Behavioral needs, 34
Binet, 83

C

Caboose, 67
California, 86
Cardboard, 65
Cerebral palsy, 137
Chalkboard, 104
Child-centered, 3
Child development, 81

Child programs, 17
Children, 17, 30, 31, 132
Children's behavior, 23
Christmas, 106
Chronic health disorders, 113
Chronological age, 57
Church bells, 125
Classroom
  activities, 32
  ecology, 24, 28, 32
Classrooms, 30, 33
Cluttering, 136
Cognitive development, 14
College
  degree, 25
  faculty, 35
  preparatory program, 8
Colleges, 34
Communication skills, 21
Community, 15
  resources, 49
Compartmentalization, 17
Compensatory programs, 21
Connecticut, 37
Conservation, 24
Construction paper, 64
Coordinated Community Child
  Care, 7
Crafts, 105
Crayons, 103
Creative play, 14
Creativity, 50
Culturally deprived, 12
Culturally disadvantaged, 110

D

Dame school education, 38
Day care
  centers, 5, 6
  environment, 6
  programs, 5, 6
Defense mechanisms, 129
Delaware, 37

Dental health, 98
Denver project, 73
Deprived children, 14
Developmental Picture Articulation
　Test, 131
Disadvantaged, 15
　areas, 47
　backgrounds, 5, 18
　child, 12, 63, 111, 113, 114, 115
　children, 6, 7, 9, 10 11, 21,
　　26, 27, 116, 117, 118
　students, 7
Discovery approach, 70, 71
Dramatization, 74
Drinking straws, 80
Dropout, 12
Dysarthria, 130
Dysphasia, 136

E

Early elementary grades, 11
Ecology, 24
Economic life, 8
Education, 3, 4
　oriented child, 55
　programs, 28
Educational
　evaluation, 84
　media, 21
　needs, 17, 43
　opportunities, 17, 49
　programs, 3, 4, 5, 7 15, 30
　psychology, 23, 90
　system, 4, 20, 22, 31
Educators, 21, 41, 45, 47, 50, 54, 84
Ego involvement, 117
Egocentric stage, 128
Elementary and Secondary Education
　Act, 9
Elementary grades, 87
Elementary school, 5, 42, 53
Emotionally disturbed, 18
Engineers, 25
Enrichment, 20
Environment, 9, 10, 13, 21, 23,
　24, 103
Environmental problems, 26
Europe, 38
European countries, 37

Evaluation, 70
Eye-hand coordination, 112

F

Family, 75
Fantasy, 62
Farm mechanization, 8
Fatalistic attitude, 13
Filmstrips, 78
Financial crisis, 25, 33
Finger painting, 104
First grade, 6, 47, 58
Formal education, 8
Fourth grade class, 44
Freedom, 60
Freshman, 32
　level, 51

G

Games, 101
Georgia, 37
Gifted, 18, 20
Grades, 50
Graduate sttudents, 51
Grammar, 59
Guidance, 61
Guidance counselor, 25, 91

H

Halloween, 106
Hand-eye coordination, 104
Handicapped children, 13, 51
Health, 59
　habits, 13
Health and safety, 94
Hearing, 97
Heterogenous grouped, 46
Higher education, 35
High school, 7, 9, 51, 53
Home, 11
　environment, 6
Homogeneous, 26
　grouping, 19, 19
　units, 19
Humanistic, 4
　approach, 5
Hyperative child, 113

I

Imitation, 130
Independent decisions, 17
Individual differences, 45
Industrial life, 53
Initial reading program, 41
Instruction, 66
Instructional level, 44
Intellectual
  development, 13
  functioning, 10
Intelligence, 62
  testing, 86

J

Jaw structures, 131
Jingles, 76
Juvenile delinquents, 20
Jefferson, Thomas, 38

K

Kentucky, 50
Kindergarten, 5, 10, 15, 49, 119,
  127, 128
  programs, 6
Kinesthetic experiences, 55
Knowledge, 11, 55, 106

L

Language, 14, 118
  arts, 54
  development, 10, 41, 123
  differences, 77
  experiences, 72
  habits, 128
  training, 127
Latin grammar school, 38
Law enforcement, 29
Layman, 110
Learning
  process, 4
  situations, 43
Linguistic style, 111
Lisp, 132
Listening, 14, 59, 70, 129
  skills, 113
Lock-step system, 103
Long range goals, 8

Lower socioeconomic level, 40
Low-income families, 7
Low socioeconomic groups, 6

M

Magazine, 75
Maryland, 37
Massachusetts, 37
Matching games, 75
Mathematical
  concepts, 63, 68
  problems, 63
Mathematicians, 24, 25
Mature preschoolers, 17
Maturity, 13
Medical background, 91
Memory span, 10
Mental ability test, 87
Mental functioning, 12
Mentally handicapped, 15
Mentally retarded, 18, 20
Microcosms, 22
Middle Atlantic, 38
  colonies, 37, 38
Middle class, 4, 10
  migration, 8
  parents, 11
Migration patterns, 8
Minischool, 49
Misarranged teeth, 130
Modern society, 48, 120
Money, 63
Monosyllables, 11
Montessori, 14
Motor
  coordination, 14
  education, 14
  skills, 56, 96
Mouth, 12
Muscle coordination, 100
Music, 14, 121, 122, 123

N

Negro
  children, 10
  culture, 12
  ghetto children, 12
New England, 37, 38
New Hampshire, 37
New Jersey, 37

New York, 37
New York City, 86
North Carolina, 37
Number, 67
Nursery schools, 5, 119
Nutrition, 98

O

Old Deluder Act, 37
Opthamologists, 56
Oral   ,
  communication, 111
  language, 59, 74, 112
Oxymoron, 47

P

Paraeducational people, 91
Paraeducational personnel, 88
Paraprofessional training, 34
Parent involvement, 15
Parental attitudes, 19
Parents, 6, 11, 14, 44, 54, 57, 58, 60, 61, 84
Peer acceptance, 19
Pennsylvania, 37
Perception, 14
Perceptual motor learning, 56
Pesticides, 26
Philbrick, John, 39
Physical
  abilities, 118
  bodies, 13
  development, 13, 94
  fitness, 96
  violence, 8
Physically handicapped, 15
Physicians, 89, 90, 91
Physiological
  characteristics, 43
  development, 55
Picture Articulation Test, 131
Play, 95
Playground activities, 29
Playgrounds, 29
Political science, 24
Pollution, 24, 26, 29
Poverty, 8, 12, 26
Pre-elementary school, 108

Pre-primers, 54
Preschool, 41
Preschoolers, 17
Preschool years, 61
Prevention, 4
Private schools, 84
Problem solving, 69
Psychiatry, 90
Psychologists, 12, 13, 47, 89, 91, 133
Puzzles, 80

Q

Quincy Grammar School, 39, 40

R

Readiness, 13, 54, 57, 58, 60, 62, 74, 87, 122
  period, 53
Reading, 41, 42, 54, 80, 81
  instruction, 44
  readiness, 41, 59, 72, 76
Reasoning ability, 10
Regular academic program, 9
Regular classrooms, 51
Remedial procedures, 82
Remediation, 4
Research, 47
Retardation, 11
Retention policy, 43
Rhode Island, 37
Rhythm, 125
Rhythmic movements, 64
Right answer syndrome, 92
Romans, 99
Rote learning tasks, 10
Russians, 24

S

School, 52
  administrators, 42
  centered, 3
  children, 107
  curriculum, 44
  education, 120
  houses, 49
  organization, 37
  population, 8, 17

programs, 117
teacher, 113
Scientific knowledge, 99
Secondary education, 35
Secondary schools, 50
Second grade, 45
Self
  expression, 102
  fulfilling prophesy, 47, 48
  image, 46, 122
Semiskilled labor, 116
Semiskilled operations, 25
Sensory
  experiences, 11
  motor activity, 55
  motor learning, 55
  stimulation, 11
Sixth grade, 45
Skin, 97
Slow learners, 25
Social
  adjustment, 50
  backgrounds, 105
  class status, 19
  development, 13
  growth, 119
  relationships, 15
  scientists, 24
  work, 90
  workers, 89, 91
Social Security Act, 5
Socially disadvantaged children, 6
Socially maladjusted, 131
Society, 13, 30
Socioeconomic backgrounds, 10
Socioeconomic levels, 47, 84
Songs, 124
South Carolina, 37
Southern Colonies, 37, 38
Spacecraft, 51
Spatial relationship, 104
Speaking, 59
Special education, 83
Special programs, 18
Special students, 18
Speech, 59, 134, 137
  defect, 134
  patterns, 115
Sputnik, 24
Standardized achievement test, 44

Standardized group tests, 45
Standards, 28
Stanford-Binet, 82
Strategies, 27
Student
  involvement, 31
  teacher, 3
  teacher planning, 32
Stutterers, 136
Stuttering, 137
Subject matter, 42
Suburban communities, 5
Suburbs, 5
Syllable, 135
Symbolization, 134
Symbols, 70, 136
Symptoms, 21

T

Taxpayer revolt, 33
Teachable time, 62
Teacher, 4, 18, 22, 27, 28, 42,
  44, 54, 60, 65, 66, 70, 124
  preparatory programs, 32, 35
Teaching, 122
  principles, 77
  styles, 29
Television, 119
Tempera paints, 103
Textbook, 47
Text material, 42
Thanksgiving, 106
Theologians, 53
Therapist, 130, 133, 136
Title I, ESEA, 9
Tonsils, 130
Twelfth grade, 50

U

Undergraduate students, 32
United States, 26, 40
Universities, 82
Unsafe housing, 8
Unsanitary conditions, 8

V

Vanderbilt University, 10
Verbal expression, 14

Virginia, 37
Vision, 97
Visual
  discrimination, 14
  memory, 78
Vitamin C, 98
Vocabulary, 14
Vocational skills, 25
Voice, 134

W

Washington, George, 38

Wechsler Intelligence Scale, 82
WISC, 83
Word rhythms, 125
Workshops, 60
Written words, 74

Y

Young children, 7, 73, 102, 105

Z

Zoo animals, 76